MW00652122

THE
COOK BOOK
OF

ALL TIME

THE
COOK BOOK
OF

ALL TIME

recipes, stories, and cooking advice
from a neighborhood restaurant

ASHLEY BERNEE WELLS & TYLER JEREMY WELLS

Photography by Christopher Morley

HARVEST
An Imprint of WILLIAM MORROW

THE COOK BOOK OF ALL TIME. Copyright © 2024
by Ashley Bernee Wells and Tyler Jeremy Wells.
All rights reserved. Printed in Malaysia. No part
of this book may be used or reproduced in any
manner whatsoever without written permission
except in the case of brief quotations embodied
in critical articles and reviews. For information,
address HarperCollins Publishers, 195 Broadway,
New York, NY 10007.

HarperCollins books may be purchased for
educational, business, or sales promotional use.
For information, please email the Special Markets
Department at SPsales@harpercollins.com.

FIRST EDITION

Designed by Su Barber
Photography by Christopher Morley

Library of Congress Cataloging-in-Publication
Data has been applied for.

ISBN 978-0-329993-1
Library of Congress Control Number: 2023936837

24 25 26 27 28 IMG 10 9 8 7 6 5 4 3 2 1

DEDICATED TO BETSY, GREG, AND CYNDY.

Thank you for all that you made us, all that you gave us.

TOMATO ON A SILVER TRAY

When you're traveling by motorcycle, certain aches accumulate: stiff knees, tight back, cramping hands, and shoulders that tense like clay drying in a kiln. A constant state of suspended hyperfocus trickles from one individual body part to the next. Ultimately it escalates into a single fatigue that begs you to stop and rest, to simply eat and drink. Now imagine the cumulative effect after riding for days on end. Simply unbooting your feet would be indulgent. Your destination's close. GPS indicates another three hours if you keep course, but it also offers an alternate path, one with a gorge known for very blue waters, so you make accommodations to stop and swim because baptism by wild waters is a specific kind of bliss. You're cutting it close, but it's summer and you're in France and in love, with the benefit of youth and the longest days of the year on your side; you don't intend to skimp.

The water soothes your tired joints like medicine from an ancient healer (maybe you're not that young, in fact). Hours pass. Wet and tired, hungrier but refreshed, you hop back on the bike and set out to race the sun to your lodging. But the ETA has moved further into the future, and the sun is sinking faster than you're driving. Cell service is long gone, but you don't speak French anyway. You pull over to reread the directions from the email confirmation for the remote, medieval stone cottage you're trying to locate by feel. In Google-translated English, it says more or less the following:

When you see the sign on the top of a mailbox, it means that you have found a parking lot! Twenty meters below is a bend where a track dig into schist rocks can begins. This track leads to the hamlet, and in any case, it is completely suitable and safe for vehicles even if it might seem intimidating should this be your first visit to the Cévennes.

After several passes over the same mountain road, no mailbox to speak of, you follow a combination of instinct and desperation down an unmarked, rocky trail of switchbacks. It is almost 10 p.m. The sky is electric—that fierce blue color that comes right before darkness wraps its arms around everything and pulls day into night.

If you can imagine all this, you can imagine our relief when we finally find the cottage; we are exhausted, dusty, sore. Ravenous. A man stands expectantly at the end of the road to greet us. Thin and tall, wearing a bucket hat and wire-rimmed glasses, he smiles through his graying beard. We are embarrassed by our extreme tardiness; his wife cooked supper hours ago. Pascal dismisses our concerns and waves us over enthusiastically, how I picture Tyler's dad would have welcomed us home.

He's over the moon to explain in admirable English the history of his three stone cottages (built in the fifth century) and to show us how he and his wife, Frédérique, have converted them into guesthouses. He points out the fence he built to keep the boars out and takes us under an ancient bridge to a twinkling swimming hole, nine feet deep and guarded by no fewer than fourteen spiders. They're harmless, he assures us, and recommends a midnight dip. Stars are now in abundance and a crescent moon hangs high, so Pascal concludes the tour. He takes us inside each of the three cottages and asks us to choose one, which is difficult because we are exhausted and they are all perfect, and making a choice would suggest that there was a lesser option, which we don't want to imply. Pascal insists. We oblige our host and select cottage number three. We are past the dinner hour even by European standards, fully prepared to fend for ourselves.

We flip open the bike's top box and dig out a half-eaten bag of mostly smashed crackers, a round of Pélardon, and the bottle of wine we picked up at the last gas station (gas stations in the Cévennes are much better than those in Los Angeles). As we arrange these items on our patio table, we are worn out, hungry, and perfectly happy to sit in the dark and eat cheese off a knife while the cicadas go on and on.

It's at this already idyllic moment that a small figure comes down the hill from the main house. It's Frédérique. She walks toward us with urgency, carrying something we can't quite yet see. She arrives on our porch and sets down an ornate silver tray. The tray is utterly beautiful; etched handles gleam in the moonlight recalling some long-ago period and an anonymous silversmith. It's a tray you'd see for thousands of dollars at an antique store or in a five-star hotel. In the center is a single tomato the size of a small pumpkin, flanked by a proper steak knife, two forks, two small wine glasses, salt and pepper in tiny glass shakers, two white linen napkins, and a little dish of olive oil. Frédérique, beside herself that we missed dinner, had gone into her garden to locate and harvest this Jurassic tomato in the dark, possibly the largest yet known to humanity, so concerned was she that we have supper. We thank her as profusely as possible given our pathetic abilities in French, embarrassed and regretful we don't speak the language, save for some bashful mercis. She hardly says a word. Her care is evidenced by, and proportional to, the colossal tomato and the inarguable elegance in its thoughtful delivery. Intuiting our needs as only a genuine host can, she heads up the hill, leaving us alone to dine.

We cut into the tomato and top it with the smashed crackers. We shake salt and pepper from their cubes and spoon olive oil over the plate. We unwrap the gas station goat cheese and set it on the tray, plunging the steak knife into the cheese without bothering to wipe the tomato juices and seeds from the blade and fill our small wine glasses with the open, not very cold bottle of rosé that was sloshing around on the back of the bike for hours, and we proceed to eat one of the most memorable meals of our entire lives.

We have had some spectacular meals, privileged in both decadence and company, but to be so loved by a stranger, so fed by a single tomato, it was an emotional event. The tomato was delicious—juicy and sweet; it tasted like earth. But the sincerity in Frédérique's gesture is what brought me to my knees.

The tomato wasn't delivered in exchange for money or credit or praise; she simply had to feed us. It's the same driving force that propelled my Jewish mother, whom I can vividly picture yanking things urgently from the fridge to assemble and heat up at 10 p.m., when I would roll home from college on weekends; it's how I imagine Tyler's dad would make his salsa, chopping onions and cilantro in his denim cutoffs, or why his mother went out to collect berries for her cobbler. It's what compels Chef Paul, while completely in the weeds during dinner service, to put a mini ceviche tostada in the pass for me, knowing I've been dreaming of that snack silently all night. I watch the line cooks put sliced melon up for the servers and I see the baristas line up lattes and mochas for the cooks—not in answer to a request but by intuition, out of care. These are the acts of service. They can't be sold or bought.

On one of our first dates, Tyler and I went for tacos. When the guacamole and chips landed, we dipped, as you do. The guac dwindled down, and we kept halving what remained

in the bowl. We each wanted the other to
have the last bite of guac. It came down to
a ridiculous extreme, a comical speck of
avocado. Sometimes when life has sucked us in
so far and I'm irritated that Tyler has used my
handmade Japanese pruning shears to butcher
a raw chicken, I recall the guacamole because
it's us at our very best, putting someone else's
comfort ahead of our own, finding real joy
through the delight the other takes in simply
eating something delicious—a lot like that
tomato. That's hospitality.

On that motorcycle trip our senses were
sharpened like carbon steel on a whetstone.
The scent of the fresh laundry and the bread
baking in each small town wafted into our
helmets. Our needs were whittled down to
extreme basics—vending machine cappuccinos
outside the restrooms at the Total were heaven,
and the ham sandwich we ate on a roadside
bench much later from the same fuel stop was
luxury. We've long since retired the bikes, but
Frédérique and her tomato stick with me as the
purest expression of the intangible thing we
work daily to create.

Collected here are our meals and stories. They
are partly mine, partly Tyler's, and ultimately
ours, intertwined as a single artifact. They
connect us. They navigate us. They shorten
geographical distances to those who live far
away and strengthen our connection to those
we love who are no longer alive.

They are the proof, the reason why pizza
bagels and quesadillas and epic tomatoes
from a stranger's garden are as meaningful
as properly searing the lamb shoulder before
a braise, as crucial as salt itself. Though a
cookbook implies a set of tool-specific tasks
and skills collected and honed over the
course of decades, preferably in a professional
kitchen, that's not what these pages, nor our
favorite meals, contain. Our recipes are not
too measured—that's not how we live and it's
not how we eat. Cooking isn't about technical

training, though a sharp knife will take you
far. It's about feeling, connecting with, and
cultivating your senses so that the memories of
the meals stain your soul and stick to your ribs
long after the guests leave and the dishes are
done (or aren't).

Make these recipes your own. Follow your
instincts. Use this book as you would a map,
not the rule of law. You can add pepper even
if the recipe doesn't say to do so; you can use
more vinegar for a dressing or throw nuts in
the cookies; you can stop for a swim in a gorge.
Cooking and eating and feeding and serving
are really just loving. That's yours to shape, to
roast, to stir, to bake, to discover—and it has
nothing to do with staying on the main road.

ON COOKING

For a short period of time, when the world was suspended and even a warm meal was only tenuously accessible, we sold market boxes filled with the good stuff we'd used for the menu at All Time—produce grown by farmers we knew, and meat and fish from trusted purveyors. The specter of the pandemic loomed over daily life. Quality goods were hard to get. Naturally, the neighborhood was excited. And then the phone started ringing. People were calling to ask what to do with a steak, or what the green stuff was that looked like broccoli, with the yellow flowers (flowering broccoli).

I realized very quickly that people hadn't been cooking much. Maybe for special occasions, but not with confidence, and not for pleasure or day-to-day living. I remember a guy who was so intimidated by the idea of cooking fish. When I told him to salt it, get a pan hot, put it in the pan, and then leave it be on the stove, he said, "That's it?!" He braced for nine additional steps and complicated instructions. To which I replied, "Yes. We're just cooking!"

I catch myself saying that a lot. I say it as encouragement to a young cook who I see panicking when we run out of bok choy for the fish in the middle of dinner service, when a pile of gorgeous purple kale sits ready in waiting; I say it in exasperation to myself, when I read about a new restaurant that's sphere-ifying a strawberry in mid-July, as though that's more impressive than whipping up some crème fraîche and enjoying the berry as it grew. I say it to no one, to everyone, to myself.

And while cooking does take effort, food can be delicious without being overly serious, and it can be enjoyable and rewarding without being intimidating. You don't need an iCombi (a fancy oven with more controls than a Cessna) or tweezers or an immersion circulator. You don't need those in your home, and I don't necessarily think you need them in a restaurant.

All Time really started in our backyard. We cooked food mostly outside since the kitchen in our home was the size of a bathroom and equally conducive to chopping onions. I built a wood oven on cinder blocks because, as a romantic, I will always prefer cooking on live fire. I love analog, simple, traditional things that work, and that you can fix when they don't. Cars, bicycles, tools, pots and pans, knives, and cooking fuel. Fire is so practical. It doesn't break. As I type this, we've had four of our six ovens at All Time go down. Three of them were brand-new and cost the rough equivalent of a medium-size yacht.

I am designed to make the most from the least. I grew up poor in West Virginia and that's certainly a part of what appeals to me. To cook outdoors, you need wood and not much else. You can build a fire grill for less than twenty dollars if you're crafty, and that's satisfying.

Fire is flavor. Dogma can come along with fancy equipment; that can yield food lacking a point of view. If you've handed over the sensory aspects and decision-making of cooking to an operating system, what's the point? Fire reacts with food and becomes its own flavorful ingredient. If you can learn how to use that to your advantage, your food will taste better.

Cooking on fire is simple. There aren't too many levers to pull, and constraint breeds creativity. Creativity doesn't come from limitless options; that's being spoiled. Boiling pasta water over a fire is creative. It slows you down to each step of the process, tunes you in. Not that you always want to make pasta like that, but you might find yourself in a place where you'd want to. Like when you're camping.

Ashley and I made hot dogs in the fireplace of a cabin in the woods that had no kitchen. I cooked a steak dinner in the same fireplace without pots, pans, racks, or cooking implements. It was a mess. It was also memorable, unlike the chicken that a computer might cook (yes, that's a real thing).

Fire also requires patience and negotiation. The inputs are so honest. More heat, more wood. Too much heat, move some coals away. Too much direct heat, raise the rack. Not enough heat, get it closer. What I've learned from cooking on live fire translates to cooking in a regular kitchen, too. I've always instinctually cooked hot and fast, of course, but learning to moderate fire has given me context and honed how I gauge heat on a stove or in an oven. I'm not afraid to get things smokin' hot, and you can replicate that to great effect with a stove or oven, if you're versed and willing.

Cooking on fire has taught me problem-solving, one variable at a time. Keep the grill height the same and adjust the fire. Or keep the fire the same and adjust the grill height. Or keep them both the same and adjust the time things cook. I don't think cooking on fire is hard, and you can use many different types of grills, or build a simple fire pit and put a cast iron or a resting rack over it; the options are endless. You'll learn fast from experience. I think it's the most fun you can have when cooking. It can be social. It can be private and contemplative. It's romantic. It warms you. After it's all said and done, your wife will say you smell like the fire, in a good way, and you'll go to bed warm, full, and proud.

I am in love with cooking on fire—and it's always my first choice—but at All Time there's no way to cook on a fire. Not more than once, anyway. We have a 36-inch (90 cm) plancha and twelve burners; there are no circulators,

no modern contraptions, just cast-iron and carbon steel pans and four committed cooks. I'm beyond proud of the food we put out.

You likely have everything you need in your kitchen to make fantastic, impressive food, and everything in this book. I'm not saying that you don't need to take care when slicing a steak (across the grain) or heating the right type of pan properly; professional guidance and good technique go a long way. But it's far less important to follow a recipe to the letter than it is to learn *why* you should temp a steak or separate dry ingredients from wet.

Our best meals were served at a table I built myself in our backyard. I kept it loaded up with pork shoulder, hot tortillas, short ribs, birthday cake, bowls of guacamole, summer corn, charred squash, whole branzino, giant salads, and rice—always rice—my wife loves rice. It was a good old table where the seats stayed warm. The food at All Time was born of those dinners and the breakfasts that followed them. We stole the recipes from ourselves to put on our opening menu, because that was the food we wanted to cook, eat, and share. We adapted the dishes to the rhythms of a busy restaurant, so they've evolved along with our guests and our team and time. This book is a homecoming of sorts, for the food especially. Only now, we're in your kitchen.

A WELL-STOCKED KITCHEN

Ingredients and Tools

I strongly believe farmers do the hardest work out of everyone in the food industry. They grow the food and contend with the ever-challenging environment, the politics, the instability. And still they provide for us. If we can basically just not mess up that effort, by enjoying the process, and feed people honestly, then we honor them. That's what it's all about. The essence of great cooking (and great food, in my opinion) is simplicity. It starts with sourcing great ingredients. That takes some research and some effort, but it's worth it. The food in this book relies on the quality of the ingredients because there are no tricks or masks.

After that, add in a couple of inexpensive tools, find a way to get things hot, throw in some basic techniques and a little understanding of why and how—now you have a recipe for a good, honest meal. When I was eighteen, my mom bought me a full set of cookware made by All-Clad. When I went to culinary school, I bought myself a Wüsthof chef's knife. I moved into an apartment in 2012 to find that someone had left a cast-iron skillet deep in the back of a cupboard. These tools are still in my kitchen today. I still use them all regularly. You don't need drawers full of gadgets (junk) to cook great food. Simply invest in a handful of quality tools when you have the means to acquire them. You will hone your skills through the process, and you'll also learn to tap into your instincts, which you can apply to anything you set out to make. Like they say with jazz, master your instrument, master the music, then forget all that shit and just play.

The following are a handful of items I suggest having in your kitchen; you don't need more than these essentials to cook everything in this book. Truthfully, you might need even less.

Chef's knife: Technically you can get away with just this one knife. You can do small work with a big knife but not big work with a small knife. Bigger is better than smaller. An 8- to 9-inch (20 to 23 cm) chef's knife will take you far. I'll admit I own a lot of knives because I like having a lot of knives (most of them are Japanese, because that's what I've grown to appreciate), but a German steel blade can take a solid beating, stay sharp, and be sharpened much easier.

Combination whetstone: Now, having a great knife isn't of much use if you don't know how to take care of it. If you take the time to learn how to sharpen a knife, well, you're doing better than most. Large vanity knife sets are not very sharp to begin with and won't take you very far. It's so satisfying to know that I can bring back a sharp edge to the handmade knife that someone left in the sink after she dulled it "tailoring" my favorite leather belt so she could wear it (not in our household, just saying hypothetically). The sharpening process is a little bit iterative, in the best way. Watch some internet videos to learn; Jon from Japanese Knife Imports in LA has a great series on how to care for knives. A combination stone and a couple different grits will do you nicely. I'd recommend a 600 grit (lower grits are more abrasive), 1,000 grit, and something in the 3,000-grit range. All in, you could have a lifetime sharpening set for less than a hundred dollars. I'll start at 600 and work up to the higher grits successively. I'm not a fan of the gizmos or gadgets that offer a quick, automated solution for sharpening knives. They are kind of one size fits none and I think you'll enjoy learning the manual way. There are few things more pleasing than working with a sharp knife. Or, perhaps more accurately, there are few things more infuriating than working with a dull one.

Cutting board: I like a thick butcher-block cutting board in end-grain wood, although they require special care and don't come cheap. An occasional oiling, sanitizing after use, and a sanding and refinishing every year or two will make a good one last forever. They're also beautiful in the kitchen. I keep a large wood one on hand for everything, and I also keep a few small (7 x 5-inch [17 x 12 cm] or so) boards handy that can be used for slicing steaks or for doing small work when I don't want to pull out the heavy board and mess up the kitchen. It's nice to mince a single shallot or slice one dry sausage on a small board and helps keep a workspace tidy.

Quality plastic cutting boards are perfectly useful, but the longevity isn't the same. There are some composite types that are thin and light and nice to work with, and especially good for smaller work. While a plastic cutting board can be a suitable replacement for wood, glass cutting boards will mess up your knife and slide and flop around mid-chop.

Pots and pans (listed in order most essential to less so but still nice to have):

1. An 8-inch (20 cm) *and* a 10-inch (25 cm) cast-iron skillet. Lodge is affordable and made well, and while I do like the fancy designer stuff, I doubt they're any better than a Lodge, which'll be an eighth of the price.

2. A 5-quart (4.7 L) cast-iron Dutch oven. Again, Lodge is a great value. Le Creuset is worth the investment, but only if you can and want to spend the money.

3. A proper saucepan. A 5-quart (4.7 L) will do you nicely. Preferably steel with what we industry types like to call a heavy bottom. In addition to tall, straight sides and a handle, it should have some heft and a couple layers of metal on the bottom, for even heat distribution. You could cook nearly every recipe in this book if you just acquired this saucepan and the previous three mentioned.

4. My next most-used pan is a 9-inch (23 cm) carbon steel sauté pan. It's sturdy like cast iron but thinner and a bit lighter. Not sure about the exact chemistry at work there (I got a C in third-grade science class and that marks the top of my academic achievements), but I make omelets, fry eggs, cook steaks, brown vegetables, make small batches of rice, and cook most things for one or two in this pan. Ours was hand-forged in a shed behind a house by a guy named Dennis Kehoe, and it's the most beautiful piece of cookware we own. This pan was a gift from my wife. She's always getting me thoughtful gifts. She also sometimes edits my writing. Lodge makes a good version of this carbon steel pan, but if you're in the mood to invest, Kehoe Carbon Cookware is truly singular.

5. A 12-quart (30.5 cm) stockpot. You could do pretty much everything in the Dutch oven, but sometimes it does feel weird to boil spaghetti in cast iron. Opt for a steel stockpot, not aluminum. They cook about the same, but you'll feel more confident with a nice steel pot in hand, and that will be evident in your cooking.

6. An 8-inch (20 cm) quality nonstick skillet. I don't know what they must do to get a pan to your door with a nonstick coating for twenty dollars, but I'm guessing it's not good. Invest in carbon steel or spend the money on an All-Clad or something of similar quality.

Now it's about to get somewhat gratuitous, but a 6-quart (5.7 L) straight-sided sauté pan with a lid is quite a treat. They are beautiful and you can do a lot with them: small braises, rice, sear, and lots of other stuff. It's a big pan, which is nice to have. But I still maintain you can get away with two cast irons and a Dutch oven.

Tongs: Get the real, rubber-less spring-loaded restaurant tongs. They're 9 inches (23 cm) long and made of stainless steel. At less than ten dollars, get two pairs. Heck, spend an extra dollar and get the ones that lock closed so they don't pop open in your drawer and jam it shut for the next eight months.

Spatulas (three types to have):

1. A fish spatula for fish and other delicate morsels. The defining features are that they're super flexible, slatted, and very thin. Especially great for taking cookies off the baking sheet. I use a fish spatula 95 percent of the time I use a spatula.

2. A sturdy metal grill spatula with a wooden handle for heavy items and anything that needs a little prying, such as a 16-pound brisket engulfed in flames.

3. Rubber spatula: Get a couple of these in small and large sizes for stirring, getting everything out of bowls, and gentle mixing. These are shaped differently than your flipper spats but thicker and rounder for scooping and scraping and such.

Thermometer: I'd suggest acquiring a decent digital thermometer that won't require constant calibration. ThermoWorks makes the industry standard, and you can get what you need for about twenty-five dollars or so.

Cake testers (for steaks and cakes): The analog thermometer, if you will. They work like this: Insert the tester into a steak for about 5 seconds; remove it and quickly touch it to the front of your bottom lip (the thermometer, not the steak). Your body is about 100 degrees, so if the cake tester feels colder, your steak isn't done. If it's the same temperature, start paying attention. If it's warmer, well, you get it. You're not in any danger of burning yourself here; really, not to worry!

We don't have a thermometer at home, and I swear by this method and use it when cooking everything from steak to roasted turkey. Of course, it takes some practice, but once you get it down you feel like a god of the culinary arts. With a little practice you can get quite accurate, and it helps you develop a better feel as you cook.

The simplest—and best—version is just a metal stick with a little plastic tab on one end. I think eight-packs cost six dollars. Or six-packs cost eight dollars. Either way, they're cheap as heck and you can use them to test cakes, too.

Vegetable peeler: I use our peeler for shaving Parmesan mostly, but of course you'll use it for vegetables, too—carrots, potatoes, cucumbers, and whatnot. I like those Swiss multicolor three-pack ones because they're cheap and replaceable. Vegetable peelers are the culinary equivalent of socks in the dryer—they constantly disappear. Even if you're sharp and manage to hang on to the same peeler for longer than a month, you should still replace it occasionally; you'll know when it's time.

Digital scale: It's very important to own a digital scale. Especially for baking. More importantly, you must use the digital scale. Volume is not accurate for things like flour, sugar, and even many liquids. In this book, some recipes are *only* given in metrics for this reason! You should be able to get a great scale for less than thirty dollars. Make sure it works in grams and can go up to at least 3 kilograms (3,000 g). Once you get in the habit of weighing ingredients, you'll never go back.

Resting rack: Restaurant-style racks are designed to fit in something called a sheet pan. It's not common parlance, but just imagine a baking sheet that lives in a restaurant. That's a sheet pan. Resting racks fit to sit perfectly

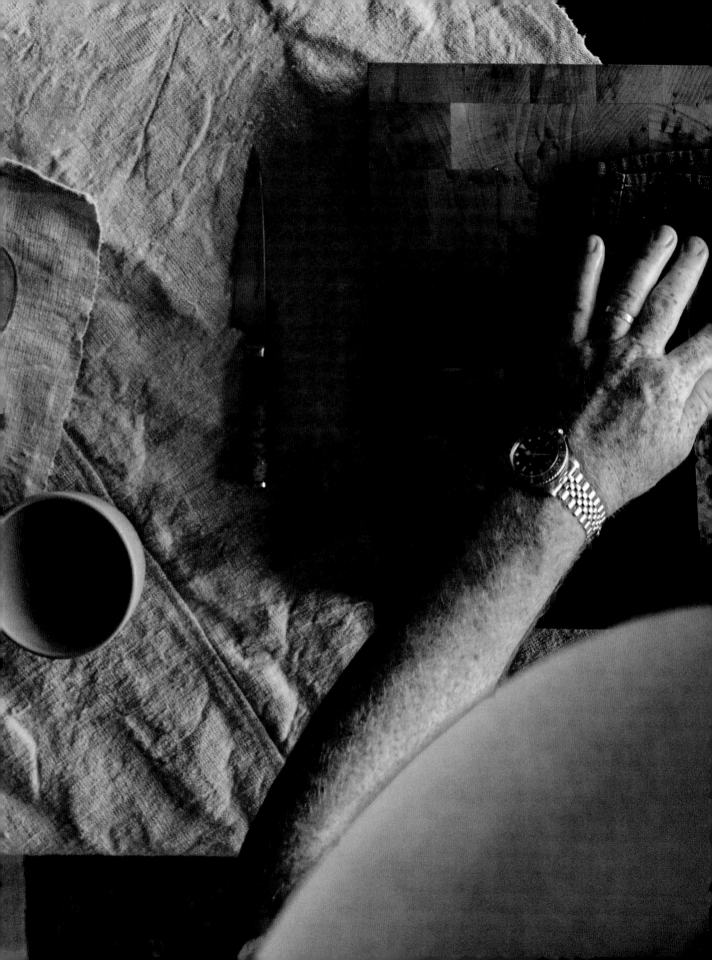

inside the sheet pan, so that air can circulate around something you might be cooling, or you can season and bring a steak up to proper temperature before you cook it without setting it flush on your counter or a plate. They come to fit standard pan sizes called full, half, two-thirds, quarter, and eighth, and this object is the linchpin of a kitchen in many ways. You'll find it extremely useful—not only to rest a steak or cool cookies, but also eventually you'll work up the confidence to set one over a burner on your stove and improvise a grill. It's thrilling. You just need two sizes, a small and a large, and it's convenient to get the correspondingly sized baking sheets, aka sheet pans, while you're at it. Two nice sizes to keep around your kitchen would be the half sheet, 18 x 13 inches (46 x 33 cm), as your large, and the eighth sheet, 9½ x 6½ inches (24 x 16.5 cm), as your smaller size.

Steak knives: The steak knives in our household (and now our restaurant) come with a preamble. I've been a cook for twenty or so years and an enthusiast for even longer, so I've always had kitchen drawers full of stuff. I like having the right tools for whatever random task may be at hand. Within reason. Though I do love my wife, I never actually bought one of those apple peeler/corer/spinner piles of garbage (Ashley once tried to convince me it was an efficient contraption). I remember the day I could buy actual nice ceramic plates for eating and hosting. Factory seconds, of course, but still, I had it all. Or so I thought.

One day shortly after Ashley and I started dating, a package showed up from France. In a linen box, with a handwritten note, were six of the most beautiful steak knives I'd ever seen, two of each in a different shade of gentle pastel. It feels like I'm writing some bad copy for a steak knife sponsorship, but it's a strangely crucial square of the All Time quilt. We have hosted more dinners in our backyard than I can remember, and in the early years, I felt proud of my factory seconds and matching

wine glasses and even the respectable silverware I had acquired. But I never owned steak knives. I guess I just figured there weren't any worth having. I served sliced steaks anyway, so who needed them, really?

These knives were not the dull, serrated version of steak knives I had seen up till then. These were sharp. And they were not serrated. Also, it was my birthday. These knives were such a gift, one I didn't even know I needed. Ashley is a talented gift giver.

The knives became a fulcrum—more of a reason to cook and have people over and gather and talk. They were showstoppers, always remarked on when we brought them out. Aesthetically stunning, yes, but they also felt so luxurious to hold—I had never encountered such a useful and beautiful object in all my years cooking and eating. And they sliced effortlessly. As I've mentioned, I am a sucker for a sharp knife.

"Imagine," we'd say, "if you could go to a restaurant and use *these* knives?" and "If we ever open a restaurant, we have to have these steak knives." This thoughtful, unexpected birthday gift set an important, early stone on the path toward All Time.

A year and a half later, All Time was born. I was working daytime in the restaurant and then going into full-time construction mode as soon as we closed in the afternoons. I would paint, tile, build more tables, and then I would I repaint and hang shelves, and on and on. Six weeks in, it was time to open for dinner service. I was nervous every day, terrified about money, sales, labor, food cost, and anything that fell outside of welcoming people and making tasty food. Which is to say, the business implications weighed heavy.

Ten days out from our first dinner, and Ashley asked me, "Soooo what about the steak knives?" You know, *the* steak knives, the ones she had gifted me that were yes, very beautiful and also painfully expensive? It should be noted that if I'm playing the financially responsible role, we're in wild times. I told her the knives were important to me, but we didn't know if dinner would even work or, hell, whether the restaurant itself would make it, so we may want to reserve that money for a refrigerator we might need or to cover some payroll and then get them down the line. My patient, thoughtful, cooperative future wife understood, and I thought that was the end of the conversation.

One night, I began painting the walls (again) at around 11 p.m. I was using a sprayer and that meant I couldn't stop until the job was done. It was one of the worst nights I've ever had—dead tired and trapped until I finished. And I had to be back at 6:30 a.m. I came home to our tiny house about 3:45 a.m., covered in paint and literally running on fumes. I tiptoed in and noticed a stack of six linen boxes and two handwritten notes: the first from Ashley, something about how proud and certain she was, and the second, scrawled elegantly, in French: "Ashley and Tyler, Good luck with the restaurant."

I'll never know how Ashley found the money for those knives. Probably for the best. But I am so grateful that she did.

These steak knives are, in some ways, as important as any of the choices we've made. They feel so representative—of our commitment to quality and our attention to all of the details. But also, they speak to the reason we opened All Time in the first place. We wanted to capture the feeling we had in our backyard, where having a meal was a special thing composed of good food and wine but also surprised you with unexpected beauty and stories around the bend.

We had six sets of those knives initially, and the servers would present the knives tableside to allow guests to choose from the pastels. At the end of every dinner service we hand-washed them, polished them, and tucked them back in their boxes like a ritual, all the while astonished that they were all accounted for. We've had to acquire more sets as we've gotten busier, and all of the boxes are worn now and carry their own story within a nesting doll of other stories. The knives have been respected by servers and runners and guests and dishwashers. Everyone has a reverence for the knives, and I still sharpen them by hand for the restaurant. We still use them at home when we have friends over, and they are truly elemental to how we dine and host. All that to say, even if you are the most casual home cook, a special set of nice steak knives brings ceremony to a meal, connects you to the purpose of cooking and sitting down to eat, and is an act of taking thoughtful care of your guests (or even just yourself) every time you use them.

A few more things before you get started
We've cited metric equivalents for units of measurement and oven temperatures for all of our friends living outside the confines of the imperial system.

Some recipes note tools that are highly specific and immensely helpful.

All olive oil in this book refers to high-quality fresh extra-virgin olive oil. We only cook with that or butter in our home and also at All Time.

All salt in recipes refers to kosher salt, except when flaky sea salt, aka fancy salt, is called for to finish a dish.

Sometimes the quantities for salt and olive oil are loosely stated, as in "a generous sprinkle" or "a glug." When it matters, we've indicated the exact quantity, but otherwise, we're asking you to feel into the process and develop your sense of seasoning and confidence, so you can begin to cook intuitively.

The same goes for serving sizes; mostly they're indicated, but sometimes you're going to navigate that with your own burgeoning instincts.

Use the freshest, best stuff you can find—meat, fish, fats, vegetables, fruit. These recipes will only be as good as the ingredients you source.

The recipes here are meant to be revisited, over and over, so you can make them your own and eventually won't have to refer to this book except to read passages aloud to your guests, for romance and entertainment.

On that note, we recommend reading through the entirety of a recipe before getting started. There are plenty of things that will be helpful to know ahead of time—and, heck, you'll just get inspired.

ODE TO VEGETABLES

Vegetables have more to offer than most people want to believe. They're not just some side dish or accompaniment. To me, what makes any dish great is that something on the plate—not the main thing—becomes the essential thing. Yes, the steak itself is delicious, but there's some kind of magic alongside it. I like to cook so that the vegetable is that magic. A spectacular vegetable is the difference between a good meal and a great one, and to me a great meal has you pushing aside a perfect piece of fish or a juicy, beautifully cooked steak to get to the Broccolini because it's just that insanely good. Vegetables have the star power. They can steal the show, but they have to be cooked properly.

I cook vegetables to coax out all the extras. Every vegetable has its own distinct flavor, a natural sweetness-to-bitterness ratio, a specific texture, a color. To preserve the integrity of what the farmer grew—the respect and love we have for the farmers we work with is immeasurable—we can't mess it up with a bunch of unnecessary process or overdo it with a million steps or drown it in an ocean of sauce. Vegetables have soul, and they must be cooked with some, too.

When I moved to California, a friend took me on a day tour of Los Angeles that culminated in a trip to the farmers market in our neighborhood. That was my first glimpse into the community surrounding food and farming, and I felt such a strong passion and energy around growing food that day. The honesty of it inspired me, and it's central to how we cook at the restaurant. Our team snaps to attention on the rare, precious occasion any farmer comes to dine at the restaurant. So whether a vegetable is eaten alone or accompanied by many other things on the plate, it must be cooked with reverence, just like meat or fish.

A hot fire is always my preference for cooking vegetables (most things, really). The real key is heat. So you need a pan that gets hot—cast iron, carbon steel, stainless steel (avoid nonstick)—and the courage to drive the temperature up. Way up. I'm talking about getting vegetables hot. Very hot.

I could fill a dozen volumes with every combination of vegetable, method, and style—there are so many options! Since you chose this book, you are no doubt bright, good-looking, and capable, so we'll share some of our favorite approaches and recipes, lay the groundwork, and then you can freestyle based on what you like, what's in season, and what your blossoming instincts tell you will work together. Remember, none of these recipes work without good ingredients—find yourself an honest vegetable grown by a farmer and work with what's in season. That's the most important step in these recipes.

CHARRED BROCCOLINI WITH CHILES AND VINEGAR

This is one of my favorite vegetable preparations. It's a great example of simple cooking that yields a lot of flavor and does right by the vegetable.

Serves 4

Extra-virgin olive oil
3 bunches Broccolini
Kosher salt
1½ smoky dried chiles (½ per bunch of Broccolini), such as chipotles or chiles de árbol, finely chopped
Red wine or white balsamic vinegar, your choice
Marcona almonds or hazelnuts (optional)

Get a large cast-iron skillet hot over medium-high heat. In a large bowl, drizzle olive oil over the raw Broccolini so it's partially coated (not drowning or sopping wet), season with salt and the chopped smoky dried chiles, and toss together.

Add the Broccolini to the pan in a single layer and allow it to cook for 2 to 3 minutes undisturbed, until you see some char and the edges start to get crispy. Flip the Broccolini with tongs and cook for another minute. Turn the heat off and add a splash of vinegar to the pan; it should sizzle and glaze the Broccolini. Now put it back into the bowl and toss to coat with any of the olive oil, salt, and chile bits that didn't make it into the pan. I like to add some Marcona almonds or hazelnuts for a little crunch; now's the time if you're into that.

You can also do this on a grill, but keep in mind that oil will drip and burn fast on a live fire. This can very easily set your food on fire, which is perhaps a little too primitive; a big fireball is not safe nor does it provide sustenance. To avoid that, wait until after grilling to dress the Broccolini. Get the grill hot and use tongs to set the dry Broccolini on it. Grill until the stalks become tender, 2 to 3 minutes, then flip them and grill another 1 to 2 minutes. Pull the Broccolini off the grill and into a large bowl to toss with the aforementioned good olive oil, salt, smoky chopped dried chiles, and a nice vinegar of your choosing, and I suggest those nuts—for texture!

WHOLE ROMANESCO

The romanesco is in a class of its own. Visually mesmerizing, mathematically perfect, it was love at first sight for me. It's just one of the coolest-looking vegetables I've ever seen. It's a sturdy vegetable that can handle a lot of heat and still retain nice texture. When you look at a romanesco, you think, damn that looks badass, because it is. I like to cook romanesco very simply using some high heat and not too much else. All hail the romanesco.

Serves 2

1 head romanesco
Kosher salt
Extra-virgin olive oil
Sauce of your choosing (optional)—any of the following will work great: Crunchy Nut Salsa (page 113), Romesco (page 77—romanesco with romesco!), or Chimichurri (page 63)

Preheat the oven to 425°F (220°C).

Trim off any wilted leaves on the romanesco but keep the good-looking ones. Halve it vertically, tip through the stem. If you perform this surgery with precision, you should have two halves. If you can't feel your legs and there's a lot of blood, call 911. Sprinkle the cut side of each half with 1½ teaspoons salt. Rub the salt in good, so it gets down to the bone. Do the same with olive oil, about 1 tablespoon per half. Make it like a Russian bathhouse: lubed and salty.

Get a large cast-iron pan hot over medium high, about 2 minutes. Place the halves cut side down in the pan. Make full contact; you should hear a sizzle. Lower the heat to medium. Use a heavy lid from a pot or a cast-iron grill press (or use the cookbooks you don't need anymore) or hold them down with your hands. Whatever you use, don't say, "But they're too uneven, I can't do it!" You can. Just get the job done. This book isn't going to tie your shoes for you, and we trust you'll figure this out. Doesn't have to be perfect, just push the vegetable down to increase its contact with the hot pan for maximum char and texture. No, they aren't going to sit flat in the pan, we're dealing with 3D models of the Fibonacci sequence. It's okay! Hold them down for 3 to 5 minutes, until you've achieved disturbingly deep color—use your tongs to check. If you are *not* doin' these up with any sort of sauce to serve, pour another 1½ teaspoons olive oil and 1 teaspoon salt over the romanesco halves, then flip them over so they are cut side up; if you do plan to dress or sauce the vegetable before serving, do not add additional oil or salt.

Put the pan in the preheated oven for 12 minutes (set a timer) and then poke one with a sharp pairing knife or a cake tester; you want it to provide a small amount of resistance—it shouldn't be hard, and it shouldn't be mush. It should be "to the tooth," or al dente. You'll know. Once there, take the pan out of the oven and transfer the romanesco halves to a cutting board. Coarsely chop the romanesco and then put the pieces on a serving platter. Now you could dress it for success with any of the aforementioned sauces or let it go nude (simple, totally acceptable). Serve alongside your meal. You should be feeling liberated by this simple preparation and the delicious vegetable you now have to eat as you please.

CAULIFLOWER

I love cauliflower. It's so versatile and really user-friendly. I find myself turning to it often, a default when I need something crunchy and vegetably on the table. This recipe can of course be applied to other vegetables, including romanesco, and you could even cook multiple vegetables together with this preparation and serve them as a delicious cornucopia.

Serves 4

2 heads cauliflower or romanesco, or one of each
Extra-virgin olive oil
Kosher salt
Unsalted butter (optional)
Red wine vinegar or white balsamic vinegar, or Pique Hot Sauce (page 100)
Chopped green herbs or red pepper flakes plus flaky sea salt (optional)

Go around the head of each cauliflower and trim it like a fancy hedge, cutting off the florets from the stem so you have about ¾-inch (2 cm) pieces that are roughly uniform in size. In a large bowl, toss the florets in 2 tablespoons olive oil and sprinkle with salt. Get a large cast-iron pan hot over medium high and have some faith.

Add the cauliflower and give it a quick shake so each floret gets a chance to make contact with the hot pan. For the love of all that is holy, don't overcrowd the pan. The cauliflower should fill three-fourths of the pan, so there's room to shake (do this in batches if you're cooking more than that, otherwise you'll end up with mush). Once your little florets are situated, splash in more olive oil or a nice knob of butter. Butter burns pretty quick, so you can always use the two together. Olive oil gives you a generous margin, as it has a higher burning temperature than butter. Lower the heat to medium.

Leave them be! Apparently, it's human nature to mess with something and move it and keep fiddling with it, and that's exactly what we aren't going to do here. If you're looking for a crispy, crunchy, perfectly brown sear on your florets, you must leave them alone. Cauliflower that's all white and mushy is boring, but so is cauliflower that's just crisp and nothing else. Do not move it around. Stoves vary but check the individual florets at about 4 minutes. The florets should be tender but not mushy. Each floret will have texture, toothiness™, and char. Once the heat is right, it's hard to burn cauliflower, trust the process.

Once there, turn the heat off and add a glug of red wine vinegar or good white balsamic vinegar, or the pique hot sauce. It'll sizzle and glaze the vegetables with acidity and sweetness, activating the superfecta: salty, crunchy, sweet, acid (another option: add a halved lemon cut side down at the beginning of cooking and squeeze with tongs at the end instead of using vinegar).

If you like, toss with some green herbs or red pepper flakes, and add some flaky salt for crunch.

BRUSSELS

As I'm writing this, autumn in LA is setting in, which just means we wear jackets and sweaters and pretend it's not still 78 degrees. It's also the time of year for another season of broiler vs. Brussels.

Many people claim they hate Brussels sprouts. It's sad but understandable. I've been to some very good restaurants that prepare them so poorly, it's unfair to the Brussels community. Let me be clear. Brussels sprouts are wonderful. You just have to cook them well. The challenge is getting them crispy without turning them to mush. To do this, we'll use the broiler. Broiling is like cooking on a hot flame from the top rather than the bottom. So the same recipe in the pan works beautifully under the broiler. The whole oven is hot, but the broiler concentrates the heat so you get color, texture, and gorgeous char on the vegetables, and fast.

And while home ovens are okay for baking cookies and somehow not much else (okay, maybe for also wasting 45 minutes heating up chicken nuggets to the temperature of the underworld on the outside and ice-cold inside so I burn my mouth because my eight-year-old self is starving and impatient and hasn't yet learned how to cook), home oven broilers are secretly, quite dangerously, overpowering and very awesome. I love the broiler. The broiler begs for forgiveness instead of asking for permission. I once knew a beautiful woman whom I now live with and have a business with and am also married to and wrote a cookbook with who had yet to understand the power of the broiler. She put something under it and set a 9-minute timer, at which point she stepped away to most likely do some study of astrology or quantum physics or similar. Nine minutes under a broiler is not unlike kissing the surface of the sun. You don't recover. Whatever she was cooking

(nachos?) could not be identified nor eaten. She now sets a 20-second timer, allegedly.

The power of the broiler can be harnessed for good. There's a reason its setting is after the 550-degree mark on the oven dial. The broiler is the inner surface of the very top of your oven, or less likely, in a drawer in the bottom of your oven—and if so, Godspeed; legally, I can't recommend you use that thing, but I bet it gets wicked hot!

1 cup (88 g) Brussels per person
1 tablespoon extra-virgin olive oil per cup
Kosher salt

(You have a few options for churching these up, so read through this recipe before getting started and choose what you think sounds good.)

Position the oven rack (before it's hot!) so it's 6 to 8 inches (15 to 20 cm) below the broiler element at the top of the oven. Halve the sprouts through the root. I used to take the root end off but I don't anymore. It's delicious and it helps hold the sprout intact, leaves together. Toss the Brussels sprouts in a bowl with olive oil and salt. Lay the sprouts out on a sheet pan or in a large cast-iron skillet. Make sure they are mostly in a single layer. A couple stacked here and there is fine, but we don't want layers.

Slide the pan under the broiler. Check for crispy edges after 2 minutes, bearing in mind that broilers are wild stallions. They're all different and you'll need to tame yours. Once you have some crispy edges and some leaves starting to brown, very carefully remove the pan and give it a gentle shake or toss the sprouts with tongs a bit to get a rotation on which ones are nearest the hot beast. This is an inexact science by design, so if you're chasing *(Recipe continues)*

uniformity just buy the modernist cookbook, quit your job, sous vide your prefrontal cortex, and kick your feet up in the VR Barcalounger. The joy of cooking—the joy of food!—is variation; unexpected bites from individual parts that make up a greater whole because they're each unto their own.

After the first shake/toss, get them back under the broiler. Now wait. Quit fuckin' with them! Dear god, I say this all the time. Let them go, another 2 minutes at a time, without disturbing them. Deep brown crispy tops are the sign they're almost done. At this point you might be saying to yourself, frantically, *I think they're burning. Are these burning?!* Then you'll know you're almost there. Go another 30 seconds. Have faith. Carefully remove the tray or pan from the broiler only after you're sure you have a safe landing spot for a hot pan. An old dish towel can only protect you for so long. Transfer the Brussels sprouts to a bowl. From here you have few serving options:

1. Drizzle Brussels with a high-quality sticky, aged balsamic vinegar; you could add some good blue cheese, even. A drizzle and a sprinkle, respectively. There's no right amount, you're honing your instincts, taste as you go. Toss to serve.

2. Add some pomegranate seeds, chopped Marcona almonds, a white or red wine vinegar, or even apple cider vinegar. Toss together! Again, feel it out by tasting it.

3. Just squeeze a lemon in, grate or peel some Parmigiano straight in and crack some black pepper over the top. Adjust as you taste. Serve it when you like it!

It's not difficult. It's not rigid. You can use the above approaches and "recipes" for most vegetables; find your dream combination of acid, sweet, salty, crunchy, texture, char, and tenderness. Taste along the way. Serve with confidence.

GRILLED FLATBREAD

We were cooking dinner for a lot of people on a farm. Everything was on open fire and I was panicked that there wasn't going to be enough food (there was enough food for another twenty people). I guessed at a flatbread recipe we could pull off in a few hours and cook over a fire. Well, hot damn it worked—a happy accident, as Bob Ross would say. We made this recipe on a wood grill, but propane works, or a cast iron on the stove. Whatever adventure you choose, the key here is that your cook surface must be hot—and remember, this bread cooks lightning fast.

There are two things you need to make good bread: (1) Develop some strength from the gluten in the flour, and (2) create an environment for yeast to get to work and make the bread rise. Normally, it takes a long time for bread to ferment and develop good flavor. For this recipe, we'll make a pre-ferment, also called a sponge, because that helps the yeast to activate quicker and imparts some nice depth of flavor.

Bread dough isn't hard, but it can be confusing. It usually rises twice and has to relax, and the steps seem arbitrary. It took me twenty years of dabbling in bread to finally connect the steps to the reasons. Hopefully it'll just take you a few paragraphs.

Okay, here we go.

Pre-ferment (aka sponge)

50 grams all-purpose, type 85, or
   bread flour
340 grams room-temperature water
9 grams instant dry yeast
6 grams granulated sugar

Dough

450 grams flour (same options as for the pre-ferment), plus more for dusting
15 grams kosher salt
40 grams extra-virgin olive oil, plus more for the bowl and cooking

To finish

Extra-virgin olive oil
Flaky sea salt
Chopped fresh flat-leaf parsley or other herbs
Red pepper flakes

In a mixer
To make the pre-ferment, whisk together the flour, water, yeast, and sugar in the bowl of a stand mixer. It will be very wet. Let it sit uncovered, fermenting, for 20 minutes. It should be a little foamy and smell yeasty and delicious.

To the same bowl, add the dough ingredients: flour, salt, and olive oil.

Find the dough hook attachment and mix on medium low until everything is together. Increase the speed to medium and use the mixer to knead for 5 to 6 minutes, until the dough is smooth and springs back when pressed.

If mixing by hand
Mix together the pre-ferment in a large bowl with a fork until it's mostly smooth. Let it sit, uncovered, for 20 minutes or so.

Slowly add the rest of the flour, the olive oil, and salt and mix with a fork until it's too heavy and sticky to keep going. Lightly flour a work surface and turn the dough out onto it. Knead the dough until it comes *(Recipe continues)*

together and becomes smooth and springy. It should take 7 to 10 minutes by hand.

Lightly oil a large bowl. Gather up the kneaded dough and tuck the edges under so that it has a smooth top and the bottom is pinched together. Place it smooth side up in the bowl. Cover with a damp towel, another bowl, or plastic wrap and allow to double in size. Depending on local temperature, it'll take 1 to 2 hours.

Once the dough has doubled in size, flop the dough onto a floured work surface. Gently press the air out of the dough and flatten to about 1½ inches (3 cm) thick. Try to press it into a shape you think you can cut into even pieces. A rectangle is ideal but not always easy. A circle that's aspiring to be a rectangle, now we're talking.

Using a pastry cutter or sharp knife, cut the dough into even-ish portions, each about 4 inches (10 cm) square and 1 to 1½ inches (2.5 to 3 cm) thick. We're making very rustic, forgiving bread here, so it's all going to be okay!

Find some clean counter space to flour (or if you're spread out like a wizard and your workspaces are all occupied by various messes, flour a sheet pan). Working with each portion one at a time, gather the edges and tuck them under into the center to form a tight ball of dough. Do it a few times, then turn the ball upside down and pinch it from the pulled-together bottoms and let it dangle offensively in midair like your uncle's prized truck nutz™, allowing gravity to assist in creating surface tension, then set it smooth side up on the work surface or sheet pan. Continue with the remaining dough portions, leaving several inches between portions for rising. Cover the whole lot with a damp dish towel. Let them relax and do their work for at least 30 minutes and up to 90 minutes. They will rise while you get a fire going (or find a cast-iron pan) to cook them.

You'll want to pour a little olive oil, sprinkle flaky salt, and maybe some herbs and/or red pepper flakes on this bread as soon as it's off the heat, so chop up some parsley and put it in a bowl, add some olive oil, a couple big pinches of flaky salt, and some red pepper flakes to combine, or you can just hit each piece with a drizzle of oil, some flaky salt, and some chopped herbs as they come off the heat one by one.

On a grill

Get a hot, mature fire made of mostly coals. Clean and oil the grates to prevent sticking.

On (yet another) floured workspace, use a rolling pin to roll one portion of dough as thin as you can get it; ¼ inch (6 mm) thick seems reasonable. This dough is forgiving and will be delicious even if it's a little thicker.

Once rolled, use your hands to lift the dough off the table and gently lay it across the grill. Try to spread it out evenly, and keep in mind the first part to touch will stick. If you work smart, you can use that point as an anchor and gently pull the dough across the grill to get it nice and flat.

The dough will puff up and get crispy on the edges and where the grill grates are, 60 to 90 seconds. If the dough is a little on the thicker side, go 15 to 30 seconds longer.

Use tongs to grab a corner of the bread and pull away from the grill slowly, making sure not to tear the bread, and flip it over. Cook another 60 to 90 seconds.

On the stovetop

Find the widest cast-iron or quality nonstick pan you have and get it hot over medium heat for 2 minutes. Add 1 teaspoon olive oil to the pan and swirl it, then put your rolled-out dough on the pan and let it lie, however bizarrely it lands; seriously, don't try to rearrange it. Give it 90 seconds, then flip it over *(Recipe continues)* with tongs. You'll see weird bubbles, crispy bits, spots that look underdone, it's all good. Let it cook 60 seconds and then use tongs to pull it off the heat and onto a rack, platter, or tray.

I like to drizzle the prepared oil mixture over each piece of flatbread as it comes off the grill. You can also just hit them with oil and sprinkle herbs and salt haphazardly. Pile them up like pancakes and people can grab a whole one or tear off part of one. This is shareable, rustic food at its very finest. It also goes with anything and everything.

CUTTING BOARD SALSA

This is a simple recipe and crazy versatile. "Salsa" is a loose term that encompasses a genre of flavors, so the real magic for this one comes from the char you get on the fresh, flavorful ingredients, brightened by good citrus and salt. My dad loved to make salsa—shirt off, denim cutoffs (great legs run in the family), so you could try that, too, and see if it has a positive effect on the end result.

Besides jean shorts, you'll need:

3 or 4 limes, halved; if limes aren't around, sub in halved lemons or oranges (char the same quantity and taste as you add each one, seeing what you like as you build the flavors)
4 fresh poblano chiles (Anaheim or Hatch chiles work, too; make sure they're fresh, not dried; use Fresnos or jalapeños if you want more spice)
2 large spring onions, halved through the root, or 8 scallions, whole, or 1 red onion, quartered, or any combo
1 bunch cilantro
1 bunch flat-leaf parsley (optional)
Flaky sea salt
Extra-virgin olive oil

Place the limes, chiles, and spring onions over a hot fire. This is best done on an open flame, but you don't need to build a fire from scratch; you can bet your sweet ass I've done this on an open burner inside our house. You can put a grill rack over the burner or do this on a barbecue, binchōtan, and even a trash-can fire. Or use a cast-iron pan over medium high or put the items on a sheet pan and use your oven broiler. Limes go flesh side down. Chiles go on whole, unseasoned and dry, as do spring onions.

Spring onions will cook the fastest—about 4 minutes (and scallions even faster!)—so remove those first. Allow the chiles to blister and puff; they'll start to turn black on the outside. This is good. Everything will be tender and blackened in about 7 minutes; if you've never grilled a lime you've been missing out; prepare to be turned on. Once everything is properly charred, remove from the heat and place everything on your cutting board.

Most people would scrape the skins from the chiles at this point, but I'm not most people. The skins add a little bitterness, which I happen to like. I also happen to be lazy, but in case you're an overachiever, here's how to do that: Put the chiles in a small paper bag while hot and let them steam for a few minutes. This will loosen their skins so you can use a paper towel to remove them easily.

Chop off the bottoms of the spring onions after they're cooked (doing this before will cause them to fall apart, so don't do that; it makes life harder).

Now, stem the chiles by holding a chile with one hand (they'll be hot so use a kitchen towel) and pulling the stem out with the other. Pile everything, except the limes, on the cutting board along with the cilantro and, if using, the parsley, and start choppin'!

Squeeze the warm limes over the top of the chopped mix, getting as much juice out as possible, then sprinkle liberally with flaky salt, add a generous glug of olive oil, and use your hands to combine it all. Use the back of your knife to slide it off the cutting board and into a bowl. Set it on the table and put it on anything and everything—bread, fish, steak, your younger brother, your first massage client. Cutting board salsa really does make everything better.

GRILLED GEM LETTUCES WITH BUTTERMILK DRESSING

I love grilling lettuces. This salad is a go-to when we're hosting at our home, or when I'm cooking an event, like a party I forgot I committed to, or some fancy ticketed dinner where I need to prove I have some tricks without getting too clever. It's fast, delicious, and impressive.

Serves 4 to 6

Buttermilk Dressing

....

½ cup (120 ml) high-quality whole-fat yogurt
½ cup (120 ml) high-quality mayonnaise, preferably Kewpie (it has a nice tang)
½ cup (120 ml) good buttermilk (something organic and from pastured cows)
White vinegar to taste
Many cracks black pepper
Kosher salt
8 chives, finely chopped
1 teaspoon dried parsley
Smoked paprika or cayenne (optional)

Grilled Lettuce

....

4 to 6 heads green or red Little Gem lettuces (1-plus head per person), halved the long way, or 2 to 3 heads romaine, halved
Extra-virgin olive oil
Kosher salt
Dash red wine vinegar
Additional salad ingredients:
   The rest is up to you. Cucumber, radishes, snap peas, and carrots for crunch are nice; tomatoes are great, red onion—fresh or pickled—and something like pomegranate seeds work well. You could use sliced or chopped apples or citrus instead—use what you have, use what's in season; three to four ingredients are all you need, and I like to keep it simple—onions, two crunchy raw vegetables, and that's it. I'm a texture guy.

Oh, and Marcona almonds are great, too. You could use sunflower seeds. Be yourself.

Make the buttermilk dressing: Whisk together the yogurt, mayo, and buttermilk in a medium bowl. Add a splash of vinegar, the black pepper, a pinch of kosher salt, the chives, and parsley. Whisk again. Taste it. You'll probably say, "Hmm, it needs something." Add more vinegar. Do that until it tastes good. You can also add a pinch of smoked paprika or cayenne; it's not about the spice here and you won't notice it necessarily, but it will deepen all of your flavors and create a pinkish hue, and that will feel fancy. Dressing's ready. Set aside for up to 2 hours until ready to use, or store in the fridge up to 4 days ahead.

Make the grilled lettuce: Wash the lettuce halves and pat dry with paper towels, but no need to dry completely, as the residual water will help the cooking process.

Drizzle olive oil liberally over the lettuces and salt them; splash some red wine vinegar over the cut sides, too.

Put the lettuces cut side down on a hot grill. The olive oil and vinegar will help them caramelize and cook nicely and also prevent sticking. Cook them without disturbances for 3 to 4 minutes, until the lettuces are nicely charred. Do not turn them! We're just cooking one side. Charring can also be done on a hot cast-iron pan or a grill. A grill is ideal, more fun, and quicker, but use what you got.

Remove the lettuces from the heat and arrange in a bowl that looks like it came from a flea market in Italy or maybe you got it from a ceramicist who took 12 weeks to make it. The tips of the lettuces will *(Recipe continues)* be charred and blackened, and that's what's special here—the flavor. It's not necessary to serve this piping hot. Scatter radishes, cucumber, and sliced red onion—or whatever you're using—over the lettuces with abandon. Spoon dressing over everything (everything in the bowl, relax) and serve immediately. Each guest should get one or two lettuce halves, to be eaten like a steak, which is to say with a sharp knife and fork (not negotiable). It's very satisfying, you'll see.

BEANS

Most of my life I'd considered beans to be food from a can, something you cooked by heating. Beans weren't bad, or life-changing, or special, just a no-fuss kind of sustenance. But beans have more to offer than that.

We have beans on the All Time menu in various ways. We started with organic, dried black beans. We'd cook them with herbs and chiles and they were tasty. With anything, I always start to compulsively wonder if we might be missing out on something, if there's a better way. I wondered that about beans.

We found Rancho Gordo and began sourcing heirloom beans with names of their own. Pinto beans became "Santa Maria pinquitos" and we discovered Mayacoba beans and black garbanzos. It was thrilling to notice the nuances between bean types—we were like flair-wearing bean sommeliers except we didn't wear pins or swish beans in our mouths and suck in a bunch of noisy air and then spit them out or anything crazy. That's grotesque. But we did begin to cook and eat beans with a new appreciation and enthusiasm.

Then I met Larry. Larry Kandarian drives his Prius from the Central Coast to the Santa Monica Farmers Market, then to San Rafael and San Francisco every week. At each farmers market, he humbly unfolds three tables and loads them up with seventy varieties of beans he grows on his regenerative, polycultural farm in the Los Osos Valley. That sounds like a lot, but he grows one thousand unique crops on his farm, including botanical herbs and different types of grains, too. He'll give you a four-hour master class on the progression of flavor and texture from black turtles to ayocote negro beans if you ask the right questions. I could fill this book with our appreciation for farmers like Larry, who are so dedicated to growing the things we often take for granted, so passionate about a food often regarded as an afterthought. The main takeaway is simple: Good beans are worth the money, for the earth and for your pantry.

Based on time, what's available, and how ambitious you may be, there are a few ways to cook beans. Keep in mind, maximum bean-cooking ambition need only be about three out of ten, because they are easy.

Personally, I don't soak. I have, but I don't. They're just too easy to cook without doing so. Sometimes people soak beans because the beans are old, so make sure you're using fresh dried beans. You could soak an old bean for an eternity but they'll still be tough in the end. Soaking overnight reduces the cook time but it's not worth it to me. There's also a method called hot soaking (make sure safe search is ON if you Google this one), whereby you boil the beans and then turn off the heat for an hour. This also seems an overcomplicated way to cook one of the least complicated foods around. I've never used a newfangled instant cooker, but I have heard good things and like the idea that you can come home to ready-to-eat beans; I'm a sucker for simplicity, and cooking beans can be poetically simple. Allot yourself about 3 hours from dried to cooked.

I use a Dutch oven, cast iron or enameled. Any large pot also works. Beans usually come in one-pound bags, so we'll use that as our base. A pound of dried beans yields a lot, so be prepared to end up with some absolutely delish fixin's to eat for the week. Here are some bean-cooking parameters to start with:

PINTO AND BLACK BEANS

2 tablespoons extra-virgin olive oil or lard
1 red onion, diced into ½-inch (12 mm)
    pieces
1 bunch cilantro stems, chopped small
1 jalapeño chile, diced
1 medium carrot, diced into roughly ½- to
    ¼- inch (12 to 6 mm) pieces
1 pound (455 g) dried pinto or black beans
2 tablespoons kosher salt
2 tablespoons red wine vinegar

Get your Dutch oven or 6-quart (5.7 L)
pot over medium-high heat. After about
1 minute, add the olive oil. Once it
shimmers, add the onion, cilantro stems,
jalapeño, and carrot and cook for 3 to
5 minutes, until those things soften and
the edges begin to get some color. Add
the dried beans and stir them. Add water
to cover the beans by at least double.
Bring the water to a gentle boil, add the
salt and vinegar, and reduce the heat to
a low simmer. Look for bubbles and some
churning of the beans, but nothing too
aggressive, because that will damage the
beans and they'll split. A hard boil will put
your beans at risk for mushiness. We want
our beans to be creamy, bean shape still
intact. I start tasting about 2 hours in. The
old standard of bean testing is to eat five in
a row. If they're all nice and creamy, your
beans are done.

If your beans are approaching done but
they're too watery, turn up the heat a
little to evaporate some liquid. If they're
too dry but need more cook time, add
some water. I err on the side of more
liquid. They'll soak it up as they cool,
and bean broth is its own special treat.
There is no exact science for the right
amount of water or seasoning, you have
to taste. I tend to under-season, so when
I warm them up to eat later I can add
chiles and flaky salt based on my mood.

FLAGEOLET, CRANBERRY, BORLOTTI, SCARLET RUNNER, AND MORE

I love varieties of white and speckled beans
with some escarole or kale stewed in at the
end, perhaps under a nicely cooked hunk of
halibut or some sausages. They're also a great
underlayment for pork shoulder or porchetta!

2 tablespoons extra-virgin olive oil
2 yellow onions, diced into ½-inch (12 mm)
    pieces
2 celery stalks, diced a little smaller than the
    onions or sliced about ½-inch (12 mm) thick
2 medium carrots, diced into ¼-inch (6 mm)
    cubes (about 1½ cups) or sliced into half-
    moons the same size as the celery
1 pound (450 g) flageolet, borlotti, cranberry,
    or scarlet runner–style beans
2 tablespoons kosher salt
2 tablespoons red wine vinegar

Get your Dutch oven or 6-quart (5.7 L) pot
over medium heat. Heat the oil for 1 minute,
then add the onions, celery, and carrots to the
pot to sweat and soften, but not to brown. Let
them go for 4 minutes. Add the beans and stir,
then add water to cover the beans by at least
double. Add the salt and vinegar, then reduce
the heat to a low simmer. Check on them for
doneness after about 2 hours as described in
the previous black bean recipe. Yes, that's it!

RICE

At one point we made rice at All Time four different ways every day. There's a fine line between not cutting corners and just being idiots. A busy restaurant with hundreds of moving parts will find ways to veer off the path sneakily, and just when you turn your attention to solve another problem, you end up with rice four ways. Inevitably the salmon bowl rice would get prepped as the crispy rice, or who knows what, and as a busy restaurant with very little space, it just wasn't efficient and it caused lots of rice confusion and mis-cookery.

The silver lining is that we have a lot of rice-cooking experience from which to draw! The only truly bad way to cook rice is to overcook it. Avoid that and you'll probably be happy.

Here are two basic rice methods. In either method, you can also add some diced onion and carrot at the beginning and cook it with stock for extra flavor.

RICE ON THE STOVE

This is the way I make rice at home. Its origins are primitive, and nearly every country in the world has its own version of scorched-bottom rice. Traditionally cooked over a fire, uncovered, this is the rice that breaks the modern rules—the ignore-package-instructions rice, the rice my wife loves and asks for most. This isn't a recipe for paella or tahdig, but it is certainly inspired by any of the many cultures worldwide that revere a crisped-bottom rice. No need to cook it over a fire, but you certainly can. Also, don't rinse the rice. Rinsing washes the starch off, and for this one we'll play to the starch's strength and use it to get the rice crispy.

Extra-virgin olive oil
1 cup (200 g) short-grain rice, like sushi or
    arborio

1½ cups (360 ml) filtered water or stock
Kosher salt

Get a 10-inch (25 cm) cast-iron or quality nonstick pan over medium heat. Add some olive oil to coat the pan and heat until it shimmers. Add the rice and stir to coat it. Add the water and some salt, give it another gentle stir, and let the rice settle into an even layer in the pan.

Let the rice come up to a boil, then turn the heat to the lowest setting so the liquid is barely simmering. Do not cover.

After 12 to 15 minutes, you'll see steam holes in the top and the liquid will be nearly gone. With a spoon, sneak a few grains and taste to see if it's almost done. The rice should have a nice bite, like al dente pasta. It will continue to cook even after it's off the heat, so aim for slightly undercooked if you're unsure. Most short-grain rice cooks in 15 minutes or so.

If it needs more time, gently add some water to keep it cooking, tasting it every 2 minutes. Now is the crucial phase: Just another few minutes and you'll achieve the great aforementioned crispy bottom.

When it's al-dente ready, turn the heat up to medium, drizzle 1 tablespoon olive oil over the rice, and let the starches that we so wisely didn't wash off caramelize and crisp up on the bottom of the pan. It'll take 4 to 5 minutes. Since you can't really see the bottom, listen and smell—you might hear some sizzling or light popping and hopefully smell the slightly sweet aroma of caramelization. Check the rice in the hottest part of the pan, usually the center, and sneak a taste to test for crispiness. The center will cook faster, so if it's barely crisp there, go another 2 minutes.

RICE IN THE OVEN

Use this method as the first step to make both Daytime Crispy Rice (page 104) and crispy rice squares (the ones paired with fish and greens on page 41)!

Rice cooks a little bit differently depending on age, processing, storage, and general rice witchcraft no one can figure out. In general, rice requires 1½ to 2 parts water to 1 part rice. This one doesn't. We don't know why, but it works.

2 cups (480 ml) cold filtered water
2 cups (400 g) short-grain sushi rice
⅓ cup (75 ml) rice vinegar
1 tablespoon kosher salt
Extra-virgin olive oil

Preheat the oven to 350°F (175°C).

In a Dutch oven, baking dish, or oven-safe pan, combine the water, rice, vinegar, and salt. Stir once to spread the rice into an even layer and cover tightly with foil.

Bake for 45 minutes. Remove from the oven and rest for 5 minutes, then slowly and carefully uncover the pan (watch out, hot steam!). This is your make-ahead rice for Daytime Crispy Rice and crispy rice squares. It also yields simply delicious, perfectly cooked rice ready to serve or store.

So, if you're not doing anything more than making rice, eat it!

For both crispy rice recipes, coat a sheet pan or baking dish with olive oil. Spread the cooked rice out using a rubber spatula. For crispy rice squares, smooth the rice out and pack it in tightly, about 1 inch (2.5 cm) thick—it has to hold together later when cut into squares and crisped (see page 41). For Daytime Crispy Rice, just spread the rice out loosely on the sheet pan or baking dish and let it dry out for 4 to 5 hours, or overnight. Allowing the rice to dry out is the key to a crispier experience.

COOKING FISH

As a resident expert on most things, I get a lot of emails asking how to do things of all kinds, because I know a little about a lot. For example, to install a Clarkman (garbage disposal) in your bathtub, you first must dismantle the auxiliary drain latch hasp.

One of the most common requests I get is, *Oh lord Jesus, how do I cook this fish?* The plea might be accompanied by a terrible picture of some unidentifiable sea creature. I'm here to tell you: Cooking fish is not hard. It can be a little intimidating, so before we go roasting fresh sardines on a hot log in the woods, let's work on some basics.

The biggest hurdle to cooking fish is that it sticks to everything. Pans, grills, sheet pans, all of it. The right tools and proper technique are the big-assist game changers that will put you on the right path. Recently, I've been learning to fly airplanes, and the entire industry seems to be predicated on acronyms for checklists. So many acronyms. Inspired, I've made one to help you remember how to cook fish:

F = find something that fish won't stick to
I =
S = spatula, flexible and thin, is key
H =

We'll look at two techniques for fish that will work for 90 percent of the fish out there.

WHOLE FISH GRILLED

I love fish cooked on a grill this way because it engages all of the senses. You get the texture and smoky flavor of the crispy skin and also perfectly cooked, tender fish inside. It creates variations in texture and flavor nuances that are subtle but simple, plus you get the satisfaction of cooking over fire and the grill marks make a visually impressive presentation. Fish cooked like this doesn't need much else at all, but I like to serve the recipe below alongside crispy rice squares (see page 41), charred Broccolini (see page 2), or a simple salad of fresh arugula tossed with lemon juice and olive oil. We're using a smaller whole fish here, but this method can also be used for whole sides of larger fish, individual portions of fish, and any shape of fish you would like to grill.

Extra-virgin olive oil
One 1½-pound (680 g) whole branzino, butterflied and deboned except for the spine, head and tail on (ask your fishmonger to do this)
Kosher salt
1 lemon, sliced into 6 thin rings, seeds removed
Handful of fresh herbs, leaves only; I like parsley and celery leaves, but chervil, cilantro, or marjoram are also nice, though not together—see what you like!

Fish spatula
Tongs
Plate or platter to land the fish from the grill

Prepare your fire and make sure your grill grate is clean and oiled with olive oil. It's important to have a hot grill with minimal flames. A good cooking fire isn't about high flames, but one with a mature, steady heat. Organize your grill so it's over your hot coals and if you're actively burning wood, keep it away from where you'll set the fish.

Season the fish with salt inside and out. One teaspoon per pound of fish is a great place to start. Stuff the lemon slices and herbs inside the fish, folding the top half of the fish closed, to restore its appearance to that of a whole fish, only stuffed with herbs and lemon. *(Recipe continues)*

Rub the outside of the fish with about 1 teaspoon olive oil and lay it on the hot, clean grill. The skin will get crispy and blister while the inside is protected from direct heat as it cooks. After 4 to 5 minutes, test if you can gently lift the fish with your spatula. Before flipping the fish, rub a little more oil on the uncooked side. When the fish releases from the grill, it's ready to flip. Often, a few spots can stick but you will sense when the skin is ready to be nudged and the fish can be turned over. Using a fish spatula as your primary flipping tool and the tongs to help guide you, roll the fish onto its other side. Don't worry if the herbs and lemon slide out a little bit; just use the tongs to tuck them back in.

Cook for another 4 to 5 minutes. The best indication of properly cooked fish is that the inner flesh will begin to flake. Check the corners near the head for flakiness. The flesh should be firm and flake apart, no longer translucent or slippery. Once achieved, use the spatula (with tongs to assist) to lift the fish and transfer it onto the platter.

The fish will continue to steam while it awaits accoutrement.

Informally, you can have dinner now. Just use a fork and scrape the meat from one side of the fish. Once done, gently lift out the head and backbone like Heathcliff and you'll have another perfectly intact side to enjoy. If you're serving two people, remove the head and tail, open the fish, and remove the herbs and the spine, yielding two sides of fish, two portions that can be enjoyed on their own or in the company of the crispy rice squares, charred Broccolini, or that aforementioned fresh arugula simply dressed with lemon juice and olive oil.

Formally, you'll need to train in fine dining for decades so you can dismantle the fish like it's a firearm from the French Revolution, serving it using only two spoons while discussing art and politics.

WHOLE FISH BASTED

This is a great technique for both smaller whole fish (1½ pounds or under), like sea bass or trout, and portions of larger fish, like a halibut steak or a nice thick piece of striped bass or salmon. You'll want to ask your fishmonger to butterfly and debone a whole fish, except for the spine, head, and tail. You could learn to do that, but it's the opposite of fun. For this recipe we'll cook a whole branzino on the stove by basting it. Some olive oil will raise the smoking point, so you have a wider window for not burning. You can go all butter (delicious), but it will burn faster. You can use just olive oil, too; you won't get that nutty, buttery flavor, but it'll still be a darn tasty fish.

One 1½-pound (680 g) whole branzino, butterflied and deboned except for the spine, head and tail on
Kosher salt
1 tablespoon extra-virgin olive oil
4 tablespoons (½ stick/55 g) unsalted butter
Optional: fresh herbs, Crunchy Nut Salsa (page 113), Cutting Board Salsa (page 25), or pair with crispy rice squares and greens (see page 41)

Medium-large spoon, for basting
Fish spatula

Ten minutes prior to cooking, take your fish out of the fridge and pat it dry with paper towels. Season the skin and inside the fish with a liberal amount of salt. Set the fish aside and get a cast-iron or quality nonstick pan over medium-high heat for 1 to 2 minutes. Add the olive oil and swirl gently. The oil is ready when it shimmers. With the skin side facing down, lay the fish in the pan away from you. It's likely to splash a little oil and it's a luxury when the splash goes away from, not toward, your bare skin.

You'll hear some sizzling noises and the fish will tense up a bit, shrinking the fish ever so slightly. That's great. *(Recipe continues)*

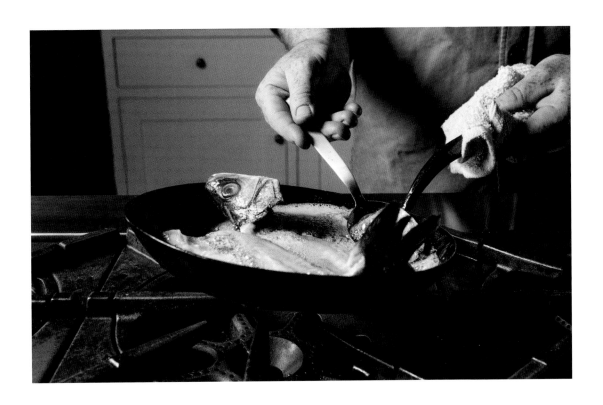

It indicates that your pan and oil are properly hot, what we're looking for. Let it cook for about 2 minutes without moving it at all; you may need to turn the heat down a bit to keep the fish cooking without burning. Stay tuned in, use your senses.

After 2 minutes, add the butter to the pan and let it melt. It'll start to foam a bit, and now we baste. Turn the heat down by 20 percent and tip the pan gently toward you, holding it by the handle at an angle. Spoon the melted, foamy butter over the fish at the top (far side) of the pan, so it bathes the entire fish, running down from top to bottom and pooling again at the little butter well in the tipped side of the pan, closest to you. Repeat that spooning technique! The butter will start to brown as the milk solids caramelize and a sweet, slightly nutty smell will perfume your kitchen. Delicious! This is the dream.

Baste the fish for 3 to 4 minutes continuously until the flesh is firm and begins to flake. Using this method, you're cooking the fish from the bottom with the flame, and simultaneously from the top with the hot butter, so you won't have to flip it.

Turn off the heat and raise the fish up from the pan with a slotted fish spatula. Tongs are strongly discouraged, as they are likely to pull the fish apart, so use a spatula. Allow the fish to drain through the spatula above the pan before setting it on a plate.

Top it with some fresh herbs, maybe some nut salsa or cutting board salsa; serve with the crispy rice and greens, or nothing at all! The browned butter will impart its own delicate flavor. Sometimes that's all you need.

FISH WITH CRISPY RICE SQUARES AND GREENS

This recipe should really be called Crispy Rice with Whatever or Nothing; the rice is the talent. It debuted on the All Time menu early on with a whole branzino basted in butter and a rotating cast of simply cooked greens based on what the farmers had at the market. It was released to much critical acclaim. You'll need to prepare the rice a day before you plan to serve this dish, using a sheet pan of oven rice (see page 35). For the original dish, serve with basted whole fish (see page 38) and sautéed greens. We discovered during late-night improv hour at the restaurant (aka family meal) the squares also work with grilled fish, vegetables, a skirt steak, or topped with fresh Ceviche (page 46)! For vegetables, revisit any of the vegetable cooking methods at the beginning of this book for practice!

One 5- to 6-ounce (140 to 170 g) portion halibut, salmon, or striped bass per person, or one 1½-pound (680 g) whole branzino for 2 people
Kosher salt
1 sheet pan oven rice (see page 35)
Extra-virgin olive oil
1 bunch of greens you like to sauté—we've used Broccolini,, Bloomsdale spinach, bok choy, baby kale, red kale, mustard greens, the list goes on, washed and mostly dried
Rice vinegar
1 lemon, halved, plus more for fresh juice
Toasted sesame seeds

Take your fish out of the fridge 10 to 15 minutes prior to cooking, so it's not ice-cold going into the pan. Dry it well and salt generously. Preheat the oven to 400°F (205°C), or 450°F (230°C) if you're planning to cook your fish in the oven only. How you cook the fish is a choose-your-own-adventure situation, so read the recipe through and hatch a game plan. *(Recipe continues)*

Cut your sheet pan of packed, dried rice into 3- to 4-inch (7.5 to 10 cm) squares. We do 4-inch (10 cm) squares. You can do whatever size, shape, or phallic reproduction that inspires you.

Get a large cast-iron pan set over medium-high heat. Add 1 inch (2.5 cm) olive oil and let the oil get hot. It will shimmer. It will sizzle if you flick a small amount of water at it (try it), and if you're using a thermometer, it should read 350°F (175°C). If it's smoking, it's too hot.

Carefully place one rice square in the oil, laying it down away from you. You don't want the hot oil to splash toward your bare arms or face! Add another square, a third at most; don't crowd your pan. The oil will splatter a little bit (if it doesn't, it's not hot enough).

A golden color should begin to develop after a few minutes. Check by lifting a corner of a rice cake with a spatula at about 2 minutes. Once it's browning, flip and crisp the other side. After both sides are nice and brown, transfer to a rack to drain. Repeat with remaining squares.

As mentioned, the original iteration of this dish was basted whole branzino. Currently we pan-roast a fillet of striped bass. By the time this book is in your hands, who could say!

If basting, revisit the recipe (page 38).

To cook the fish in the pan and finish in the oven, preheat the oven to 400°F (200°C). Set a cast-iron or ovenproof nonstick pan over medium-high heat. Add a glug of olive oil. Once it's shimmering, place the fish in the pan, skin side down, laying it down away from you so it doesn't splatter at you. Cook it for 4 minutes on the stove, and then put it in the oven for another 4 minutes. Check for a nice flake and a golden color on the top for doneness; you won't need to flip the fish. Start your greens while your fish is in the oven, and keep an eye on it.

The cooking processes may overlap a bit, but you should be able to manage!

To cook your fish in the oven, put your empty ovenproof sauté or cast-iron pan in the oven at 450°F (230°C) for 10 minutes. Coat the fish with olive oil, salt it, and place it skin side down in the hot pan. Roast in the oven for 6 to 8 minutes, until flaky. Cook the greens while it's in the oven!

To make the greens, set a medium sauté pan over medium high and add olive oil. Once the oil shimmers, put the greens in the pan and sprinkle with salt. Move them around with tongs to coat. Put the lemon halves, flesh side down, in the pan to char up and caramelize. After 2 to 3 minutes, remove the lemons and set aside. Once the greens are half-wilted, maybe 3 to 4 minutes, turn up the heat and splash in some rice vinegar or a squeeze of fresh lemon juice. It'll sizzle. After about 30 seconds, taste them for doneness and seasoning. Adjust if needed. The greens should be tender but with a toothy bite and a vibrant acidity, and nicely salted but not overly, so that the flavor of the vegetable shines through.

Plate the rice, add the greens on top of that, then balance the fish last like it's Act II in "O" Cirque du Soleil. Finish with sesame seeds and take a selfie together. Or retain your dignity and eat your meal without a care in the world. This is a show-off dish, and the crispy rice is the talent. Don't forget to squeeze the charred lemon over the whole thing. Congratulate yourself!

BURRATA ON TOASTY BREAD

If All Time had a family crest, burrata would be front and center. It's a staple recipe on the dinner menu, and we couldn't ditch it if we wanted to. Internally, it was once referred to as the Ikea of dishes because it was all assembly, no major cooking. So we were going to just illustrate a recipe for you without written instructions whatsoever and mail you an odd number of different-size wooden dowels in a plastic bag, but we worried you'd end up with Swedish meatballs. Now we bake our own bread fresh, a feat I never would have believed possible—another example of Tyler's optimism (à la minute "projects" that turned out quite successful). We never planned on keeping the burrata long-term, but it's garnered a massive fan base. Every time we consider taking it off the menu, we eat one and it is, indeed, shockingly delicious. I guess cheese and bread have been turning people on for centuries, and we don't need to challenge the fact. When fresh tomatoes aren't flavorful due to the season, we oven-dry them so they're around all year.

Extra-virgin olive oil
1 large slice (per 4 people) fresh sourdough bread; it should be insultingly thick (if it's coming off a normal boule-shaped loaf, a 2½-inch-thick [6 cm] slice is right)
Flaky sea salt
5 to 6 ounces (140 to 170 g) burrata
1 cup (145 g) cherry tomatoes, halved, or 2 coarsely cubed heirloom tomatoes
High-quality aged balsamic vinegar
Fresh Italian basil, perhaps from your garden

Get a cast-iron pan over medium-high heat and coat it liberally with olive oil. Drizzle olive oil on the bread slice, too, a sort of belt and suspenders approach. When the oil is hot, shimmering but not smoking, lay the bread in the pan, oil side down. Do not mess with it. Lower the heat to medium. Let the bread become toast. How? By leaving it be. Cooking is about leaving things alone, a skill best practiced to hone. After about 2 minutes, check to see if the bottom is golden brown and crusty. If it's not, give it more time. If it is, coat the other side with olive oil, flip the bread, and do it again.

Put the toasted bread on a plate. Slice it into four portions now—you won't pull that off once you start assembly. Not a mandatory step, but a good one if you're sharing. After you slice, arrange the bread on the plate to look like the original, intact slice. Sprinkle the bread with flaky salt and spread the burrata over the toast with a spoon; once you realize a spoon is ineffective, use your hands. Make it look as nice as possible, which is to say, it will look messy. Now scatter the tomatoes over the burrata. Sprinkle with more flaky salt, drizzle the balsamic, then drizzle with olive oil. It should be a glossy scene, all the good stuff pouring over the edges of the bread. Pull the basil leaves from their stems (do this last so they're fresh and aromatic) and adorn them across the tomatoes like you're arranging a bouquet. Serve while the bread is still warm, it makes all the difference.

CEVICHE

Ceviche isn't really a difficult thing to make. The most important ingredients are confidence, the freshest of each item possible, and a very sharp knife. Ceviche is based on the very cool idea that you add citrus to raw fish and it cooks. The acid cooks or cures the fish, which is incredible if you think about it, because it's so easy, but if it goes too long or you mix it too aggressively you will end up with horribly textured overdone fish—it's awful. Make this one as close to eating it as possible. The work is all in the prep, since really you just mix the ingredients together and that's dinner. Or an appetizer. Or snack. Or one of us at the pass annoying Chef Paul in the middle of the dinner rush asking for a single tostada, because we are all addicted to them.

Serves 4

8 ounces (225 g) tuna, albacore, hamachi, striped bass, sea bass; all will work, what matters most is freshness, which is paramount for texture and flavor, and for your health!
½ large cucumber
½ red onion
½ serrano or fresno chile; jalapeño works, just use a whole one
2 avocados
Extra-virgin olive oil
4 to 6 corn tortillas
Flaky sea salt
3 limes, plus more as needed
Kosher salt
15 to 20 fresh cilantro leaves

The fish should never be precut, not even a few hours ahead. Before you go cutting up the fish, be sure that it's cleaned (without guts, scales, skin, eyes, teeth, and head) and you are about to serve. You should be able to buy a steak or loin in said cleaned state. Using a sharp knife for even, smooth slicing, cut your fish into ½-inch (12 mm) cubes, then put these in a medium bowl in the fridge. Keep the cut fish in the fridge until the last moment, taking it out when you're ready to mix and serve the ceviche.

Dice the cucumber, onion, and chile as small as you can. Try for brunoise and brag to your friends. The goal is to get each ingredient the same (tiny) shape and size! Set each diced vegetable aside. Halve and pit the avocados, then dice each half into cubes about the size of the fish, or slightly larger; you can slice them in their skins and scoop them into the bowl with a spoon—handle it as little as possible and put it in the fridge while you make the tostadas.

Get a large cast iron hot and add ½ inch (12 mm) olive oil to the pan. Once the oil is hot (about 3 minutes or when it reaches 350°F/175°C), add the tortillas to the oil, working in batches if necessary, and let them crisp and bubble for about 90 seconds; flip them with tongs, then go another 1 minute. Pull them from the oil with tongs, placing them on a paper towel or a resting rack, and sprinkle with flaky salt.

Remove the fish from the fridge. Add your diced cucumber, onion, and chile to the fish. Juice the limes into the bowl and gently mix with a large spoon until combined. Don't abuse the fish by overmixing. You don't want to disfigure it and lose the nice cubes you worked so hard to achieve. Add the avocado last and fold with a spoon to combine, being careful not to mash it. In case you can't tell, overmixing is the kiss of *(Recipe continues)*

death. This dish relies on tasting the clarity of each ingredient within the composed whole. Taste it and add kosher salt or more lime if necessary. This dish should be brightly acid forward, with lots of punch.

Spoon the ceviche onto the tostadas while they're still warm (or use the ceviche as a dip and go full-on lazy). Garnish with a tiny bit of olive oil and the cilantro leaves. You could also use store-bought plantain chips, or anything that pleases you, for dipping. I even heard about a guy (me) who bought tortilla chips from the store and ate straight out of the mixing bowl.

CELERY, POTATO, AND PICKLED PEPPERS SET FOR WHOLE FISH

We eat about eighteen meals a week at our restaurant (a testament to our offerings? laziness?), so sometimes we burn out. But whenever we travel, we're extra excited to get back to our food. Once when I left town, I returned to an incredible new dish on the menu. It was the octopus, and while the octopus itself was great, this little set was the showstopper. The more I ate, the more I had to have, like those perverse Turkish delights from Narnia and just as sinful, only tasty. And addictive! You'd be hard-pressed to top this gem in both versatility and independence. It stands on its own, and it goes with everything; it's perfect on a pork chop, a whole grilled fish, or in a giant bowl served as a punchy salad. Of course, it's also delicious with octopus, but cooking octopus at home requires a lot, including the difficulty of handling a hard-to-acquire fresh whole octopus and many steps, not to mention the riot it would likely incite because of some heartbreaking documentary. We recommend having a nice dinner instead of an argument or a kitchen covered in tentacle trimmings.

Feel free to adjust the vinegar to your liking. We use aged sherry vinegar, which lends some extremely bracing acidity, lots of it. You could use a milder vinegar or scale back if it's blowing your face off, but the acid is what makes it sing. The pickled Juanita peppers are briny and sweet and a little spicy, which I also just love. You could use piquillos (still tasty) or roasted red peppers in a pinch (not as good).

Serves 2

---

1 pound (455 g) fingerling potatoes
Kosher salt
Extra-virgin olive oil
2 celery stalks, thinly sliced on a long bias

1 shallot, sliced as thin as you can across the root end (the short side)
¼ cup (25 g) pickled Juanita peppers, often found under the brand-name Peppadew, sliced roughly ¼ inch (6 mm) thick
2 tablespoons good-quality sherry vinegar (we use 25-year-old vinegar; quality is the mandate here)
2 teaspoons flaky sea salt
½ bunch of the freshest arugula you can find; red Russian kale is a great substitute, or just up the celery and use the leaves if you don't have good greens handy
1 whole fish (fillets also work), grilled (page 37) or oven-roasted (page 42)

Put the potatoes in a large pot, cover them with cold water, and add 2 tablespoons kosher salt. Bring to a boil. Reduce the heat to a simmer and cook until the potatoes are pretty tender but still firm enough that they won't fall apart, 10 to 12 minutes. Drain the water and spread the potatoes on a baking sheet to cool for at least 20 minutes and up to 4 hours.

Preheat the oven to 450°F (230°C).

When cool enough to handle, gently press the potatoes about halfway down with the bottom of a small pan or your hand. The idea is that the potatoes hold together but are slightly smashed.

Drizzle the potatoes with a tablespoon of olive oil, season with 1 teaspoon kosher salt, and slide the baking sheet into the oven for 20 to 30 minutes. It's pretty hard to overcook these so use your intuition—in 15 minutes they should start to become golden and sizzle; when they are deeply golden brown and look fried, they're done. This could take 20 minutes, or it could take longer. Personally, I lean long on cooking them, as everything else in this salad is raw. If you're not getting *(Recipe continues)*

any color, select the nuclear option and turn on the broiler. Just keep a keen eye on them, checking every 2 minutes and rotating them for fast, intense color.

While the potatoes are cooking, place the celery, shallot, peppers, vinegar, and flaky salt in a large bowl and toss so that all ingredients are dressed. Once the potatoes are cooked, add them to the bowl and toss to dress.

Just before this one hits the table, add the arugula so it stays green and vibrant and doesn't wilt too soon. If serving with whole grilled fish, you can place the salad on top of the fish or on the side, but either way you end up with a nice combination of crunchy, crispy, warm, and cold with a big sting of vigorous acidity to everything.

STEAK DINNER FOR ONE!

I find few things in my life more rejuvenating than fixing a steak dinner to eat alone. I love to sit at a restaurant bar and do this, especially when I travel. This steak dinner is that type of experience—a little self-care, a gesture of independence, and some peace and quiet for once. These are my general principles: I like to use just one pan, a cast iron; Strangely, I like either a small steak or a really big steak. Sometimes 5 ounces (140 g) steak is just perfect and sometimes a 24-ounce (680 g) ribeye is what you have and that'll do nicely. More on that later, but the choice depends on the kind of day you had and the meat you can get—quality is more important than size. If you're going large, you get leftover meat to make steak and eggs the next morning or share with your hound; make one vegetable and keep it simple; shaved Parm is nice, and a lemon goes a long way (my wife taught me that).

Steak of choice
Kosher salt
Fresh cracked black pepper
1 bunch escarole or a vegetable of your choice: chicories, Broccolini, cauliflower, romanesco, carrots, potatoes, or just simply a few handfuls of fresh arugula you'll season with lemon juice, olive oil, salt, pepper, and a drizzle of balsamic (you'll need good aged balsamic)
Flaky sea salt
Unsalted butter, if needed
Extra-virgin olive oil
Balsamic or red wine vinegar or juice of ½ lemon
Real Parmesan (aka Parmigiano Reggiano)

Come home and greet the dog (surely you picked up a marrow bone for him when you were at the butcher?). If the steak has been in the fridge, take it out and temp it on a resting rack for at least 10 minutes and up to 30 minutes after you season it—liberally—with salt and pepper. That's industry speak for "Let it go from fridge-cold to less cold"—so it cooks evenly! It will also brown and form a delicious crust much better.

Wash 80 percent of the dishes already waiting for you in the sink.

Pour yourself a glass of wine to keep you company while you cook.

Find a 10-inch (25 cm) cast-iron pan, a basting spoon, some tongs; hopefully these items are among the clean 80 percent.

I love chicories, particularly escarole. They wash just like lettuce, so float them in water (instead of running water through them) so any sand or dirt shakes loose and sinks to the bottom. You don't have to dry them well; you're not making a salad (the spinner can stay jammed in a drawer where it doesn't fit, even without the lid and you haven't found that since the last time you used it months ago). Set them aside; it's time to cook your steak.

Get your pan over medium-high heat and prepare to smoke up the house a bit (open a window?).

If a steak has a fat cap, I like to cook that part first. Holding the steak with tongs, press the fat cap into the hot pan so it renders. Now you can cook the steak in its own tasty fat. If there's no cap, no problem, just add a tablespoon of butter or olive oil to the pan and let it get hot for about 2 minutes, taking care not to burn it. Turn the heat down to medium and set the steak in the pan, away from you so you don't get splashes of hot fat on your arm or face. If it doesn't sizzle and you aren't a little scared, your pan isn't hot enough. Once you set it down, do not move it. Young cooks can't grasp this concept; they just want to keep checking and *(Recipe continues)*

fiddling with it. Leave it alone for a number of minutes, according to steak size, indicated below. Cook time depends on the size of your steak, of course. After the first side has a golden crust, turn it over and reset the hourglass:

4 to 10 ounces (115 to 280 g): 2½ minutes per side

11 to 16 ounces (300 to 450 g): 3½ minutes each side

17-plus ounces (480 g): 3 minutes per side twice, plus basting (see The Very Big Steak Event, page 58)

At this point you should have a crusty, seared, delicious steak and a kitchen full of smoke.

Take your steak off the heat and let it rest, on a resting rack over a plate. If you don't have a thing like that, you can tuck a fork or a spoon under your steak to prop it up so some air can circulate around it while it rests. The key is the resting. An okay-cooked steak that's well-rested will be much better than a nicely cooked, poorly rested steak. Go 10 minutes minimum and up to 20 minutes, if you cooked a big fella. Whatever you do, don't rest your steak in a hot pan. That's not gonna work no matter who you are, though mostly my wife is a pretty great cook.

While it's resting, wipe out any of the cooking remnants from the pan, but don't clean it too well. The steak fat left in the pan will impart depth of flavor for what's next. Increase the heat to medium high and add your vegetables. Chicories will cook in about 4 minutes— they'll wilt softly, while keeping some crunch. Romanesco cut into small pieces will take a little longer, but would also be delicious, as would Broccolini, potatoes, or cauliflower—lots of options. Sprinkle a little kosher salt over the vegetables, but go easy, as you salted that steak with courage and too much salt ruins a meal. You can always finish with flaky salt at the end if you think it needs a boost. Once the vegetables are browned and cooked (don't

let them get too soft), splash in some nice balsamic or red wine vinegar, or squeeze a half lemon into the pan. Toss with tongs and turn the heat off.

Wake your steak from its restful state to slice— across the grain! Put it on the plate next to the vegetable you chose. I like to slice the steak as I eat, personally. Use a vegetable peeler to shave some Parm over the plate without much precision. Eat it standing in the kitchen or in the yard, or while you grade papers or watch *Seinfeld* reruns.

THE VERY BIG STEAK EVENT WITH CHIMICHURRI AND PROPRIETARY A(LL TIME)-1 SAUCE

The first night we ever served dinner at All Time, there were just three items on the menu. Ashley and I weren't even engaged yet, but we decided in four weeks' time to open a restaurant together. After four weeks of serving breakfast, lunch, and coffee, we decided it was high time to begin serving proper dinner.

Setting up for dinner service is always a scramble, even once the wheels are greased with habit and systems. We had a few obstacles our first night, one being that the first would-be dinner service landed on Valentine's Day. No pressure. Also, our "chef" (guy who sold weed out of our kitchen as his primary job) had an emergency (had to go snowboarding), so he couldn't be there opening night (or any other thereafter).

But the plan was in motion, and nothing was going to hold us back. We activated our perennial bail-out plan (our friend Ryan). Years ago the three of us (Ryan, Ashley, and I) all worked together on a clown ship of a restaurant opening, where we solidified a lifelong friendship against all odds. The hard times we shared eventually turned into good stories, which cemented a professional respect for one another, the kind forged through laughter and tears and sixteen-hour days. In the face of less-than-ideal opening conditions, we called him in to help us get organized and run the kitchen that night. I had assured Ryan that this time the "little favor" we needed was different from that last project that had worn us all down, because we were in charge now! We'd pay him. We're a real restaurant. Things were ready. Orders were done. Prep was done-ish. We needed him only for a few hours. Those are what I like to call truthful lies. Ashley will claim she can tell by my voice when I'm telling one of these, but she can't.

Of course the fish arrived full of bones and guts and scales. The ribeyes weren't trimmed or portioned. The stations were not set up. We didn't have printed menus for guests. Eight minutes before the start of service, this six-foot-four man (not me, Ryan) was crammed under a shelf at our tiny prep sink, scaling and removing fish bones that most people don't even know exist. He was also cursing.

Well, you know how memory is. It's hard to remember the details from so long ago, but I know we made people happy and fed them well. I'm also sure lots of mistakes got made, but that's life and also cooking. There's a strange kind of comfort in accepting the fact that things won't come out perfectly, but the obstacles and bumps in the road do really fortify your kitchen skills, service instincts, and friendships. The essence of that first night is still imbued in the restaurant today. If Ryan ever speaks to me again, he would probably agree on all fronts. That's a joke, of course; he remains in our lives, kissing us both on the lips to greet us, as generous and enthusiastic as ever. Key items from that night's menu are still on the menu to this day. Details change with the seasons, but the fish with crispy rice and greens, the burrata, and, of course, the Big Steak Event are always on. It's time you learn to make one yourself.

Get yourself a big steak. We use ribeyes. Usually 36-ounce (1 kg) bone-in bad boys. You could also get a thick-cut New York, which I love. This recipe is for a ribeye because that's how we do it at All Time. Hopefully you have a powerful fan; we do, I installed it myself. If you're not going to crack open a can of drywall in your ceiling to ventilate, at least open a window in your kitchen and point the fan out of it. It's about to get smoky.

Gather:

....

24- to 36-ounce (650 g to 1 kg) ribeye or
    T-bone steak
Kosher salt
Fresh cracked black pepper
Extra-virgin olive oil
4 tablespoons (½ stick/55 g) good (pastured,
    European-style) unsalted butter, like
    Plugra
1 sprig rosemary
Chimichurri (page 63)
Proprietary A(ll Time)-1 Sauce (page 64)
Flaky salt

10-inch (25 cm) cast-iron skillet
Medium-large spoon, for basting
Resting rack that can accommodate your
    huge piece of meat

Season the steak with salt and pepper and let it stand at room temperature for 60 to 90 minutes. If you're short on time, some is better than none, even 20 minutes will help.

Set a 10-inch (25 cm) cast-iron skillet over high heat. A giant steak will cool your pan down pretty quickly, so get it hot for 2 minutes. Rub the steak with about 1 tablespoon olive oil. It'll be less messy and less scary-splashy than adding oil to the pan.

Very carefully lay the steak in the pan, setting it down away from, not toward, you. After 1 minute, reduce the heat to just above medium. The steak needs to cook a few minutes on each side, so find a temperature to brown, not burn. You'll know it's right when it smells good and keeps sizzling but doesn't burn.

Let it ride. Go 4 minutes from the time you turn the heat down. Turn it over and go 5 minutes on the other side.

Now's a good time to check the temperature with a thermometer or cake tester.

Depending on its size, you're looking for about 110°F (45°C). Any less and you'll want to cook it another minute or two on each side. If it's hotter, baste (the next step) for less time.

Turn the heat down to medium low, then add the butter and about 1 tablespoon olive oil to the pan. Set the rosemary sprig on top of the steak. Orient the pan so the handle points toward you and you can hold it to tilt the pan so that the butter and oil pool toward the handle and you.

Keep the heat on and spoon the melted pool of butter over the steak. You'll know the heat is right if your butter browns and foams and is clearly cooking the outside of the steak as you baste it. If it doesn't, add a little more heat until it feels good. If it's too hot, you can add a little more oil to cool it down or pull the pan off the heat for a minute to reset. Do this forty times, and then flip the steak and do it again. Yes, go for around eighty bastes. Let's call it ten bastes per degree of temperature. That theory is based on my own personal proprietary kind of science, which is to say, instinct. What's important is that you go for it. We're not basting three or four times for show. If you have the balls, meaning the fortitude, meaning the endurance, to baste a steak from 80°F (25°C) to 120°F (50°C), it will be the best steak you've ever eaten. Your arm might get tired, but hey, that's cooking. After basting, check the temperature again. I like to pull the steak to rest at around 120°F (50°C). There's a lot of momentum and it will continue to cook while it sits.

Once you're there, place the steak on the resting rack where it won't get cold but can rest undisturbed with some air circulating for at least 10 minutes and up to 20 minutes.

I've said it too many times and I'll say it again: *A poorly cooked steak that is well rested will be better than a* *(Recipe continues)*

perfectly cooked steak that isn't properly rested. Do not rest your steak on a hot surface of any kind. But don't be hasty. Steaks need rest.

For serving, I like to run my knife along the bone and remove that first, and then slice the steak across the grain. Serve the bone with the sliced steak, in good company with chimichurri, the AT steak sauce, flaky salt, crispy potatoes, and charred Broccolini.

CHIMICHURRI

This one is not a hard thing to make at all, but "Can I get a side/pint/wagonload of chimichurri?" has become a common request from dining guests, even ones not eating the steak. It's true this condiment is lovely, not just on steak but also on fish, vegetables, pork, rice, and even simple greens. We make it fresh with each steak, chopping everything by hand in order to maximize brightness and so the herbs and acidity stay fresh. Our recipe is surprisingly simple, fast, and easy.

Makes about 1 cup (240 ml)

1 bunch flat-leaf parsley
1 large shallot
⅓ cup (75 ml) red wine vinegar
1 lemon
1 teaspoon red pepper flakes
1 teaspoon kosher salt
½ cup (120 ml) extra-virgin olive oil

Cut the bottom 2 inches (5 cm) of the parsley stems off, and then chop the whole bunch coarsely with the stems on, so it still looks like parsley. Peel and slice or mince the shallot—it doesn't have to be uniform, and it doesn't really matter too much as long as you're getting pieces that are a lot smaller than the whole shallot. Add the parsley and shallot to a bowl with the red wine vinegar. Juice the lemon over the bowl, add the red pepper flakes and salt, and add the olive oil last. Stir to combine, then taste and check the levels—salt, heat, acid—and once you're satisfied, pour the chimichurri directly over whatever or whoever is closest to you, and then bite it.

PROPRIETARY A(LL TIME)-1 SAUCE

Paul invented this sauce, and though we've never been a steak sauce family, this stuff is one hell of an upgrade for your meat. According to Paul, All Time's Big Steak Event needed a steak sauce and since Paul has mad special sauce skill, it's no surprise he came up with this. The recipe is a culmination of sauces from his storied past; it's inspired by the A-1 variety and it sure is delicious. It works on many things, including vegetables, and certainly all kinds of meat, like a New York or a ribeye or a kookaburra (just the wings). This sauce is no rules, just right. Like Paul.

Makes about 2 cups (480 ml)

½ cup (120 ml) plus 2 tablespoons water
½ cup (120 ml) plus 2 tablespoons red wine vinegar
⅓ cup (75 ml) Worcestershire sauce
¼ cup (60 ml) fresh-squeezed orange juice
⅓ cup (75 ml) ketchup
⅓ cup (75 ml) Dijon mustard
⅓ cup (75 ml) port
½ teaspoon celery seed
½ teaspoon kosher salt
½ teaspoon ground black pepper
½ teaspoon onion powder
½ teaspoon garlic powder
3 tablespoons tamarind paste

Put all the ingredients in a 2- to 3-quart (2 to 2.8 L) saucepan and whisk together before setting it over medium-high heat to bring everything up to a soft boil. Reduce the heat to low and let it simmer for 10 to 15 minutes to develop flavor. You're not really reducing, just letting the ingredients come together. Taste it. If it's delicious, great. Adjust if you think it needs salt or anything else. Pull it off the heat and let it cool. Store it in a mason jar or something airtight in the fridge for up to a week if you don't drink it all on night one.

QUESADILLA INTERLUDE (FOR MAKING UP)

Now this recipe is based on fiction, as nary a disagreement has been had in our household, let alone anything that warrants the need for "making up." If there had been such an incident, would a melty, salty, cheesy, crispy snack top a traditional reconciliation? I wouldn't know. It's never happened. But if I had to guess, here's what I'd advise doing:

Open the fridge and see what you have. Tortillas are a must—corn, flour, spelt, kamut, whatever you got. I like corn. More importantly, so does she.

Cheese is the other ingredient. Something that melts is ideal. Something in a green shaker or can is not ideal. Let's assume, for the sake of argument (you're at capacity for that, remember), mozzarella, Jack, cheddar, Oaxaca, string, or any combination of cheeses therein works best.

You'll also want some salt—the fancier the better; we need to impress here. This is a Maldon household and we've never disagreed on that.

Get a pan. Cast iron or quality nonstick.

1 tablespoon unsalted butter
2 tortillas per quesadilla you intend to make (scale up for serious turmoil)
⅓ cup (40 g) thinly sliced or shredded cheddar cheese or pulled-apart string cheese; no shame there, it still requires effort
Large pinch of that fancy salt

Get the pan medium hot over medium-high heat.

Add the butter. It should melt immediately and threaten to burn if you don't put a tortilla on it fast.

Put a tortilla on it fast.

Sprinkle the cheese to cover the tortilla—do it sloppy so a little spills out the side.

Add the other tortilla on top. Give it a little gentle press the way lovers do to make sure they join in the holiest of unions, as they need to go from separate items to one loving being.

After about 90 seconds, take a peek and see if tortilla number 1 (presumably the transgressor) is nice and brown. If so, flip the quesadilla with a spatula or by tossing the pan like your favorite Food Network personality.

Cook the other side until it looks the same. By now some cheese should be falling out of the tortillas and crisping up since you so recklessly sprinkled it everywhere. This is the best part, don't be afraid of it.

Slide your finished product onto a cutting board and cut into eight pieces, like a pie. Sprinkle with the fancy salt. Serve it and be honest about what a jerk you were.

GOOD-ASS SALAD AND THE INFAMOUS DRESSING

When we opened the restaurant, we declared that a legitimate salad would be a founding principle. Not some frilly, over-thought delicate thing where four leaves of lettuce are arranged on a plate around a single tangerine segment or three strands of fennel that look up longingly from the plate because they can't even be scooped up with a fork. We wanted salad in a bowl. A big one. Filled with lettuces and vegetables that crunch, and fruit if it made sense, and seeds; a salad that had to be served with tongs, and so large that your jaw would be exhausted if you took it on alone; a salad that could make the rounds at the beginning of the meal but remain on the table throughout and be revisited when the main dishes arrived. Enough with artful, tiny "salads." We wanted the salad to feel like home, and at home we make giant salads and sometimes they have almonds in them and sometimes they have raw pepitas; sometimes they have apples and chunks of raw white cheddar. We've streamlined things at the restaurant because that's what you do, but the basic premise still applies: lots of crunchy lettuces, a nut or a seed, some fruit if it's fresh and in season, and the lemony dressing that everyone has come to crave, lick off a spoon, demand the recipe for, ask for more of, and make up rumors about: *It has seven types of vinegar! There is more sugar than olive oil! It's got cocaine in it*—all hogwash. The salad is yours to create—start with lettuces and add whatever else you're excited to include and can get that's in season and fresh. You don't need much, just fill it with your passions then toss it in this dressing.

1 cup (240 ml) fresh lemon juice
¾ cup (180 ml) extra-virgin olive oil
2 tablespoons sugar
1½ tablespoons Dijon mustard
1 teaspoon kosher salt

1-quart (1 L) mason jar with a lid

Yeah, that's it. Mix everything together in the jar if you have one handy, use an immersion blender (at the restaurant we do that, but not at home), or blend it in a blender. Pour it on the salad and toss to serve. Store any extra in the fridge for about 1 week. Olive oil will separate when cold, so just stir or shake to reincorporate before using it.

SHALLOT DRESSING

I used to go to my best friend's house on weeknights during elementary school because my mom worked late. They always made a giant salad for dinner, with this dazzling dressing that I thought was homemade. Turns out it was a Paul Newman joint, Italian-style flavor, but I didn't know it then, the same way I didn't know a Shirley Temple was just 7-Up and grenadine, and both retain their mystique to this day. I would drag my finger across the plate to lick every last drop of that dressing. It was punchy—so much acid and flavor! I still chase that effect in a dressing. This recipe is probably well-known in some form or another; it's my personal riff on the Newman's Own stuff. I consider this a base recipe that's already perfect as is, but you can definitely add a lot to it—Parmesan, parsley, red pepper flakes, for example. If you do, it'll be even more extreme on flavor, and sometimes that's okay.

1 shallot, minced (convince your husband to
    do it if he has more efficient knife skills
    than you)
¼ cup (60 ml) red wine vinegar
¼ cup (60 ml) apple cider vinegar
½ tablespoon kosher salt, plus more to taste
1 tablespoon Dijon or grainy mustard
1 lemon, halved
Freshly ground black pepper
½ cup (120 ml) extra-virgin olive oil

1-quart (1 L) mason jar with lid

Put the minced shallot in the jar. Pour the vinegars over the shallot and add the salt. Let it stand while you do something else. The longer you let it go the better—the shallots sort of pickle—but you can't mess it up, so don't worry too much. Add the mustard, the juice of both lemon halves, some black pepper, and anything else you plan to, pouring in the olive oil last. Shake it up with the lid on. Mustard is a great emulsifier—it hangs well with oil for a more unified dressing. You'll have crunchy bits of shallot, black pepper, and the dressing will be like its own meal, in a way. This will keep in the fridge for a week or so, and goes on plain lettuces really well, but a salad is a place to express yourself, so do it up.

WATERMELON SALAD

Tyler invited me over for Fourth of July one year, when we were in the friend zone. I don't know if that was our first official date, but no one else showed up (he called them all off), so it was just the two of us there, eating a steak with our fingers, drinking some very fancy wine, and enjoying this particular watermelon salad. I fell asleep in his hammock before sundown, and I never went back to my place again. That's a true story. This salad is impossibly easy to make, almost embarrassing to put in a book. It's become a favorite on the summertime menu at All Time, and it definitely recalls some very high romance for me. You can do lots of variations; that fateful July I think we peeled Parm and used balsamic, but this one calls for white vinegar and feta. It's a good salad because you don't have to be too rigid about it, just find some highly sexual watermelon, fresh herbs, an appropriate cheese, and the fireworks will follow.

1 small to medium watermelon, any kind,
    just as long as it's ripe and crunchy, and
    very cold; for a larger melon, use additional
    shallot and vinegar
1 cucumber, cut into large, uneven chunks
White balsamic vinegar
1 shallot (red onion works, too), thinly sliced
2 limes
French feta cheese
Flaky sea salt
Fresh mint
Fresh basil

Cut the watermelon into large cubes and put them in a medium bowl. Add the cucumber and pour about 2 tablespoons vinegar over the watermelon, then add the shallot and squeeze the limes in. Spoon gently to toss. Garnish with some crumbled feta, flaky salt, and fresh herbs. Taste and adjust, then eat! That's it.

CHEF PAUL INTERLUDE

(voice of Sam Elliott)

Sometimes there's a man. I won't say a hero, because what's a hero. But sometimes there's a man who, well, he's the man for his time and place. He doesn't fit in, but he's the exact right fit, and that's Chef Paul at All Time.

All Time went from possibility to opening day in less than five weeks. It happened so quickly that there wasn't time to stop and think, or to calculate a whole lot, or to worry about the things you should worry about when opening a restaurant. We built it fast; we shot from the hip. The restaurant was born in a state of perpetual motion and hasn't stood still since. We drive by instinct, we move at speed, and we figure any decision we might want to reconsider (plenty) can always be painted over. Many have been.

As such, All Time has embodied lots of different iterations of self. We did a take-out restaurant next door in our prep kitchen, which featured a rotisserie; we broke the rotisserie a couple times and then bought a pizza oven. We turned the whole enterprise into a grocery store and a takeaway restaurant for a couple of years. We added seating and built a bar and refinished the walls and planted many things and reworked other things when "circumstances" (global pandemic, harebrained ideas) called upon us to do so. We serve breakfast and lunch every day. We have very good coffee. Dinner is romantic with a serious wine list that's fun and full of surprises. We change the dinner menu frequently. We have about half of the refrigeration space we need and no freezer to speak of. The prep area is too small and the building is underpowered and the equipment is secondhand. And then there's dealing with ownership (us): "Our bread vendor had to close so we're going to start baking our own sourdough for the entire menu of a restaurant that's open from 8 a.m. to 10 p.m. We'll start tomorrow."

Being a chef is hard work. Being a chef at All Time would be a suicide mission for most. We have had several people inhabit the role. Each of them added their stitch into the tapestry that is present-day All Time, sure, and even the mistakes and hard times are a valuable part of the whole. But All Time is a hungry beast, and her dish of choice is a chef. We needed a leader, a swords person of the stone, someone willing to kiss the frog and allow it to become what we knew it could.

Paul comes in. And he's different. He's British and also from Florida and has the driest humor you've ever encountered, but that's not what we mean by different. His approach to improvements, organization, quality, consistency, and integrity is unmatched because it isn't up for debate: It just is or it isn't. And with him, it always is. Every system, routine, recipe, and standard that Paul has implemented falls lockstep in with the values we hold dear. And we didn't even have to ask.

Like all men of his ilk, he has a bruised past of underappreciation: he has cooked on the line, plunged toilets, protected the cold stock when the fridges went down like he owned the place, found melting outlets and plucked them nearly alight to save the restaurant from burning down; he's given loyal decades to other people who never deserved him.

We hope we deserve him.

Words can't explain how beautiful it is to see Paul in action just being Paul. He's the secret favorite of all the farmers at the market.

Our vendors drop off special samples to get Paul's opinion before they choose to stock the items. Farmers have even asked his opinion about what they're going to grow the following season. Even we (visionaries, aka opinionated people, who always think we know better) take his input very, very seriously. He runs food to tables and knows the regulars. He is a man of hospitality, a family man, and a badass cook to boot.

You could say the term "chef" has lost gravitas in the last few years. The prospect of being a TV star has waned, and the pandemic stole whatever was left of the false shine. Being in a kitchen just means working hard. These days, you could be called chef if you simply show up to work the day the other chef decided to move to Austin or got sent back to jail or decided to start a dumpling company out of a bathtub. It's not that there aren't still real cowboys out there, but the number of Stetsons on the streets don't accurately speak to the facts.

But here is a man who has actually been at it for decades. He's worked his balls raw roping in the chaos. He settles the dust we've kicked up and makes things better wherever he goes. He's a guy who has quietly learned the actual business, built relationships, standardized (written down) recipes, implemented order guides, called bullshit on an accountant because he understands a P&L and knows to the nickel how much he spent on seafood that week. He's a man who uses finishing salt with grace and effortlessly makes a plate of food look thoughtful, but only once it tastes really good; a man who, somehow, has taken the loose idea of fresh, local ingredients and the simple vision of feeding people well and turned that into something meaningful, something better than it ever would have been without

him. He does it with ungreased wisdom and perfectly timed jokes he lets out once a year.

Yep. That's Chef Paul. And to him, boy howdy, are we ever fucking grateful.

SWEET POTATOES WITH ROMESCO AND HERBY GREEN SAUCE (FOR EVERYTHING)

These Japanese sweet potatoes have become such a favorite at All Time that here we are writing a recipe for basically one simple ingredient. They have a huge following. Cult-like, even. Sweet potatoes themselves are so versatile you can adapt them to just about any style of food and pair them with almost any dish.

We use the Japanese sweet potatoes, which are on the smaller side with red skin and white flesh. There are lots of varieties out there, and the cooking method stays roughly the same, but the starchiness and flavors will differ and you'll have to monitor your cooking time according to size, so try a few and see what you like!

JAPANESE SWEET POTATOES

2 pounds (910 g) Japanese sweet potatoes from a trusted farmer
2 tablespoons kosher salt
1 tablespoon freshly ground black pepper
Extra-virgin olive oil
2 teaspoons finely chopped chives
1 teaspoon flaky sea salt, for finishing

Preheat the oven to 350°F (175°C).

Potatoes grow in the ground so it's best to scrub them up and even buff them with a kitchen towel before cooking.

In a large bowl, toss the uncooked, clean potatoes with the salt, black pepper, and olive oil.

Spread the potatoes on a baking sheet or in a large cast-iron pan so they lay flat. Bake for 20 minutes, then test with a sharp knife, cake tester, or thermometer. They should give a slight resistance but have some crushability. Home ovens vary wildly so it could take up to 40 minutes. The key is to cook these beauties to about 75 percent done, not too soft.

Once achieved, rest the potatoes for a few minutes, until cool enough to smash them. Press them into what I call half-flat. They'll still be hot, but it happens fast and probably isn't too dangerous. We restaurant folk live on the edge, so we use our palm, but you can also use the bottom of a small pot, a tiny cutting board, a plate, or whatever you see when you look around that makes you say to yourself, *Yeah, that'll work*. It's nuanced, but aim to press them down but not too flat; they should be about ¾ to 1 inch (2 to 2.5 cm) thick.

Increase the oven temperature to 450°F (230°C), toss the potatoes in another glug of oil, add another sprinkle of salt, spread them out on the same baking sheet, and bake for another 10 to 15 minutes, until the edges are crisping up so fine you say "damn." The skin should start to brown and the edges will have a visible sizzle. Your sweet potatoes will now have delicious crispy bits and a piping hot creamy interior. They should smell like whoa and are now ready to serve.

You can end the work here and slide them as is under a steak, a roasted chicken, next to some fish. For the complete, famed version, you'll want to make the below sauces while the potatoes roast so that at the last moment you can slap some fresh romesco and herby green sauce on them like a fine Jackson Pollock, sprinkle some chopped chives and flaky salt over the whole piece, and once everyone is done signing autographs, enjoy the glory.

ROMESCO

Romesco is one of those things that's different from town to town. It's a *(Recipe continues)* sauce that suits me because I like to flip open cupboards (and leave them open so when Ashley comes in she asks what kind of poltergeist came over and why they so rudely did not close the cupboards) and figure things out. I also love a sauce where the easy-to-good ratio is high to very high. It comes from Catalonia and by the time it gets across the pond it can be a totally different expression depending on who, what, where, how. Normally you'd blend in day-old bread to thicken it up. We're out here in Hollywood and somewhere between 2011 and 2022 bread became the antichrist, so in order to do well by our good gluten-fearing Angelinos, we don't use any. Come to think of it, this sauce is also traditionally made with almonds, but then with the nut allergy thing potentially killing people, we've deleted those as well. All that to say our recipe is a true bastard, but it sure is healthy and impressive and most folks can safely enjoy it. Maybe we ought to change the spelling of "romesco" to something with entirely different letters, since we've changed all the ingredients. Here's how to make the delicious bright orange sauce we know you love, the one we have historically slathered on Japanese sweet potatoes but which also honestly goes well on most anything (fish, meat, regular potatoes, charred vegetables, burn victims, your bare chest before a workout).

Makes about 1 cup (240 ml)

1½ (16 ounce) cans of roasted piquillo peppers
¾ cup roasted pepitas
5 tablespoons good red wine
5 tablespoons fresh lemon juice
Salt to taste, about ½ to ¾ tablespoon

You can use a mortar and pestle, or a food processor, but it will be a little chunkier. We make a lot of this and put it on a lot of things, so we're a blender family.

Put everything in a blender on medium high for 30 to 45 seconds, then scrape the sides with a rubber spatula and blend for another 30 seconds or so. The sauce should be smooth and slightly pourable. Give it a taste and ask yourself if it seems balanced. You shouldn't taste any one ingredient as a standout, but rather the alchemy where 1 + 1 somehow equals 8. It should have acidity, texture, depth, and saltiness all in balance. If not, add what's missing until it tastes good. Worst case is that you keep adding things until you have a double batch. Keep it in a jar in the fridge for 3 days or so. Probably irrelevant because as I said you can put it on everything.

HERBY GREEN SAUCE (FOR EVERYTHING)

One of my first jobs was at a little restaurant in Pittsburgh. It was in a wholesale district known as The Strip and I hated it, so I quit, then I went back to work there and loved it. You can do a lot of growing up in two months. Anyway, we made a lot of little sauces that stuck with me. This one is an evolved version of some other sauce I don't remember anything about except that it was good and somehow influenced my mind to arrive at this sauce here. I love remembering an old pal of a sauce, even when the two things probably have little in common. Paul and I were cooking back in the deep, in the flat circle of time called 2020, and we needed something herbaceous. At one point we just kept stuffing green things into a blender, and that's the key with this one. You can actually fit like six bunches of herbs in a blender. It came out great.

As with most things, feel free to adjust for your preferences regarding cilantro and also what you may have on hand. You know we use this sauce for the Japanese sweet potatoes alongside the romesco, but if it were socially acceptable, we'd drape it over 85 percent of the menu.

Makes about 2 cups (480 ml)

1 bunch cilantro, stems and all
1 bunch parsley, stems and all
1 bunch green or spring onions
1 serrano chile, top sliced off
1 cup (240 ml) buttermilk or heavy cream,
   since no one ever has buttermilk on hand
1 cup (240 g) sour cream
1 tablespoon kosher salt

Stuff all the greens in a blender along with the serrano. Blend on medium low to try to chop it all up a little bit. If you have the stuffer rod that came with the blender, stuff 'em in! Don't worry about blending too much at this stage, you're doing a pre-blend. *Pre*emptive because we just want to prevent the dairy from being in the blender too long and heating up, which isn't ideal.

After the pre-blend comes the main blend, so add the buttermilk and sour cream along with the salt. Start on low and turn it up to high over about 5 seconds. Once everything is combined go another 5 to 10 seconds depending on your blender. You want the herbs nice and bright green; too much blending will bruise them and turn everything brown and sad and no one wants to pay for therapy over herbs.

Give it a taste and see about the seasoning and flavors. Add more herbs, spice, salt, or liquid to suit your preferences. Keep it in a sealed container in the fridge for up to 5 days. The dairy is cultured so it actually has a somewhat long shelf life.

TOMATILLO SALSA

Tomatillo is my very favorite salsa. Like the breakfast burrito it's married to, this green salsa has been on the menu since day one and hasn't changed at all. It's easy, goes with everything, and can be used in lots of ways—you can braise a pork shoulder in it or use it as a base for soup. You can also use the same recipe below, but without cooking a thing, to make a delightfully fresh bright green salsa. That comes in handy for summertime when you don't want to turn on an oven, and works well on grilled steak, meaty white fish, black beans, and any kind of tacos.

Makes 2 to 3 cups (480 to 720 ml)

2 pounds (910 g) tomatillos, husks removed, rinsed and cut in half
1 jalapeño chile, stem removed and halved the long way
½ red onion, diced in large pieces
2 limes, halved, plus more as needed
1½ tablespoons kosher salt, plus more as needed
½ bunch cilantro, stems and all

Preheat the broiler. On a rimmed baking sheet, lay out the tomatillos, jalapeño, onion, and limes, cut side up, and put it all in under the broiler. After about 4 minutes, the tomatillos should look dark around the edges and slightly shrunken. The jalapeño and onion should begin to have some deep color. Let them broil another few minutes—some char is good, just pull the baking sheet out before everything burns completely. Grilling also works and gives a nice smoky flavor. Instead of using the broiler, grill all the ingredients and follow the same technique. Tomatillos will stick like hell to the grill, so plan to lose a few.

Let the baking sheet cool while you assemble your blender or food processor. Toss the charred tomatillos, jalapeño, and onion right into the blender. Squeeze the limes to get the juice and pulp, the good stuff, into the blender. Now add the salt and start blending on low, slowly increasing speed to avoid a hot salsa explosion. Blend for 30 to 45 seconds, add the cilantro, and blend for another 20 to 30 seconds. Adding in the cilantro at the end preserves its brightness. You can skip blending and do a rough chop with a knife to yield a chunkier, very flavorful salsa instead. Just chop the cilantro before adding it in and tossing it all together in a bowl.

Give it a taste, adding more salt and lime, if necessary. Jar it up and keep it in the fridge for up to 1 week.

ALL TIME BRAISED PORK SHOULDER

This simple dish exemplifies how we cook. Pork shoulder is a ubiquitous term for what's called a primal cut. It's a big piece of meat that breaks into an upper and lower part (the picnic shoulder and the Boston butt). For the restaurant, we buy boneless pork shoulders and cut them into pieces about the size of a baseball. They cook a little quicker that way, have more surface area to crisp up, and are easy to serve. I like to cook bone-in at home, cooking the primal cut whole first and then cutting it up after.

So, get a pork shoulder—a good one—from a place that treats its pigs well: lets them be outdoors and only gives them one bad day. It's not easy, but do your homework when sourcing meat (or anything, really).

One 3- to 4-pound (1.4 to 1.8 kg) bone-in whole pork shoulder, or boneless shoulder cut into baseball-size pieces
Kosher salt
Freshly ground black pepper
Extra-virgin olive oil or bacon grease
4 limes, halved
2 jalapeño chiles, chopped
2 yellow onions, cut coarsely into large chunks
1 tablespoon whole peppercorns
One 355 ml glass bottle of Mexican Coca-Cola (1½ cups) per 4 pounds (1.8 kg) meat
Paul's Carolina Sauce (recipe follows)
Braised Collards (recipe follows)

Preheat the oven to 500°F (260°C) if you're using a whole shoulder, or 325°F (165°C) if you're using boneless. Temper the meat at room temperature for around 30 minutes, make sure it's dry, and salt and pepper generously. About 1 teaspoon kosher salt per pound of meat is a good plan. For a bone-in shoulder, score the fat with a sharp knife, in a cross-hatch pattern.

If you are using a Dutch oven, everything can be done in one pan. If you don't have a Dutch oven, reread the intro to this book. You can use a sauté pan for searing and a baking dish for roasting, following the rest of the directions as normal.

First, we need to sear. If you're going the whole-shoulder route, put the shoulder fat (scored) side up in the Dutch oven, and slide it into the 500°F (260°C) oven to get it nice and crusty, about 10 minutes. Once it's golden and properly seared, pull it out and reduce the oven temperature to 325°F (165°C).

For boneless, you'll sear each baseball-size piece on the stove. Get the Dutch oven (or sauté pan) on high heat. Coat the pork pieces in olive oil (or some bacon grease, if you're the kind of person to keep that on hand). Sear in batches, not all at once, carefully adding a few pieces at a time to the hot pan so you don't cool the pan too much. Rotate each piece so that all surfaces get a nice crust, then remove and set aside on a plate or rack while you sear the remaining pieces. Once all the pieces are seared, lower the heat to medium, carefully wipe out the Dutch oven (or pull out the baking dish), and place the pork into it like a single-layer pork puzzle. The pieces should be touching in one layer.

After you've seared, tuck the halved limes in between the pork pieces or around the whole shoulder, then add the jalapeños, onions, peppercorns, and Coca-Cola. Add water to just barely cover the pork. Put the lid on the Dutch oven (or cover the baking dish tightly with foil) and carefully place in the oven.

Set a timer for 3 hours. At 3 hours, carefully remove the lid or foil. The pork is done when it pulls apart easily with a *(Recipe continues)* fork. Fork-tender, that's your cue to remove it from the oven.

You could stop here and let the pork cool before storing it in the fridge for later use, or, if continuing, turn on the broiler, transfer the pork from the cooking liquid to a baking sheet, and crisp it up like carnitas, about 2 minutes per side under the broiler—a nice treat!

You'll want some greens or something to go with the pork, so braise some collards or sauté whatever green you have on hand (kale, Bloomsdale spinach). We use collards on the dinner menu sometimes because Chef Paul is Southern. It takes longer, because you have to braise them, but it's worth it.

PAUL'S CAROLINA SAUCE

Make ahead or concurrently with braised pork.

Makes about 1 cup (240 ml)

1 cup (240 ml) distilled white vinegar
¼ cup (60 ml) organic ketchup (preferably without high-fructose corn syrup and/or corn syrup)
¼ cup (60 ml) apple juice
2 tablespoons plus 1 teaspoon brown sugar
2 tablespoons red hot sauce (ours is homemade; see page 103)
1 teaspoon salt
1 teaspoon red pepper flakes
1 teaspoon dried oregano
¼ teaspoon garlic powder

Put everything into a large pot. Bring to a boil, reduce the heat, and simmer to desired thickness. It really doesn't take long! Under 20 minutes. Store it in a jar or airtight container in the fridge.

BRAISED COLLARDS

Wash the collards, using around a half bunch per person. Shake them off, but don't worry about drying them well—we're braising. Get a Dutch oven on high heat with some olive oil and about ½ cup (120 ml) Carolina sauce (recipe precedes) per whole bunch of collards. Add the collards, give them a good stir, turn the heat down to low, and pop the lid on. Braise for about 30 minutes. The stalks should be tender, with a wilted leaf but not beat up.

If you don't have that kind of time, we'll cook a different green (kale, mustard greens, spinach); get a cast iron over high heat, add some olive oil, then add the greens and salt them, then use your tongs to adjust them and coat. Turn the heat to medium high for 2 minutes so they start to wilt, then raise the heat back to high and splash a little of the Carolina sauce in the pan for flavor and a glaze. The greens should be ready in 3 to 5 minutes, when the stalks are tender and the leaves are gently wilted.

Put your greens on a plate with some pork, and it's nice if you made some grits or rice to go with it, or perhaps some white beans, but if not, no shame in eating pork and greens. Pour Carolina sauce over all of it to finish.

GLAZED AND NOT GLAZED BRISKET

To me, a beef brisket is a nice thing to braise during the fall and winter months. I don't braise a lot in the summer, but you can sure as heck smoke a brisket in the summer. I did that annually for Ashley's birthday for many years. We smoked some during the pandemic with a smoker we bought on craigslist for seventy-five dollars that performed according to its price category with a little help from some user error—is it possible someone set nine whole briskets ablaze in the parking lot because they were set fat side down? Can't say. Records from this era are sealed.

To the point, there are plenty of books on smoking brisket that will all serve you better than my instructions (past experience), which could result in an out-of-control grease fire, food on the ground (probably because it's on fire), and honestly just wishing you hadn't committed to cooking for that wedding at that really expensive house in that area that was zoned high risk of fire before the cooking even started.

So yeah, we're using the oven. For legal reasons.

Pasture-raised animals are usually a bit smaller, so the briskets are also a little smaller, coming in at 12 to 15 pounds (5.4 to 6.8 kg), which is still huge. There's a fat end, the point, and a leaner end called the flap. It's the natural separation point and each side will cook a little differently. A good market or butcher can break it down for you.

One 5-pound (2.3 kg) pasture-raised beef
    brisket (you can have the fat trimmed but I
    rarely trim mine; your butcher will be happy
    to trim yours)
Kosher salt
3 yellow onions, cut into medium dice
3 carrots, peeled and halved the long way, then
    cut into about ¾-inch (2 cm) half-moons

3 celery stalks, halved the long way and cut
    into about ½-inch (12 mm) pieces
1 bottle (750 ml) decent red wine, something
    good enough for drinking
1½ cups (360 ml) decent balsamic vinegar, like
    $9-bottle decent
2 tablespoons whole black peppercorns
Filtered water

Preheat the broiler.

Season the brisket a day or at least a few hours ahead, 1 teaspoon kosher salt per every pound (455 g) meat. Place the brisket in a straight-sided roasting pan with plenty of headroom or in a Dutch oven, if it fits under the broiler. Let it broil for about 6 minutes per side, flipping it with tongs to get it browned and crusted all around. If some fat renders off during searing, that's okay.

Once seared, add the onions, carrots, and celery to the pan, then put it all back under the broiler. Stir the vegetables around the brisket every minute or two. The brisket will continue to brown and that's what we want. If you're worried it's getting too much color, you're probably doing it right. If that doesn't allay your fears, you can take the brisket out of the pan and set it aside while you continue to brown the vegetables alone and let them get some color around the edges.

Pour the bottle of wine into the pan. It should bubble and reduce a little bit right away. Slide it back under the broiler for about 2 minutes. Then remove the pan and set the oven to 300°F (150°C).

If you took the brisket out of the pan because you were afraid, carefully add it back now, pour the balsamic vinegar in, add the peppercorns, and fill the cooking vessel with enough water to just barely cover the brisket. Carefully (and tightly) cover the pan with foil, or if you're using a Dutch oven, put on the lid. Gently slide the brisket back in the oven and set a timer for 4 hours. Do something productive.

After 4 hours, very gently peel back the foil. Attention! There will be steam and steam is hot! Some evaporation has happened and now a little brisket iceberg should be poking out of the sea of future sauce. I like to poke it with a fork to see if the brisket is tender and pulls apart. It shouldn't offer much resistance, like if you had to pull a piece off with a fork and snack on it, you could. Depending on the brisket, the oven, and Mercury's position relative to Saturn, it'll take 4 to 6 hours. Keep going until you have achieved this degree of tenderness.

Once you're confident it's done, you have a couple of options. The easiest option is to remove the brisket from the liquid with tongs, let it rest for at least 30 minutes, and then start eating it in between two slices of white bread. File this one under "unglazed."

The harder, but arguably better and more impressive option, is to reduce the braising liquid into a glaze-sauce. A "glauce" or "slaze," if you will. Should you choose to accept the mission (it's actually not very hard at all), we'll just need to separate the fat that's rendered from the sauce. This step is nearly impossible, but you have to try. You could transfer the liquid to a shallow pan and let it cool on an ice bath, which could help the fat separate faster, but maybe not enough to be worth it. Skim the fat from the liquid with a ladle or large spoon. Discard the fat you can get, maybe the top 1 inch (2.5 cm) from the liquid, and accept the fact that you're not going to get it all.

Once the cooking liquid is separated from the fat as best as possible, pour it into a saucepan over medium-high heat and reduce the liquid. You want to reduce it by half, or until it has enough body to lightly coat the back of a spoon, whichever happens first.

A braised brisket will stay plenty hot for at least 1 hour, and it's important to let it rest for at minimum 30 minutes, so you should have time to make a glaze, cook some vegetables, make some polenta, or butter some noodles for the meal.

When it's time to serve, keep in mind this was all for nothing if we don't cut the brisket right. The grain of the meat changes about halfway through a brisket, so if you cooked a whole one you'll have to change the direction that you're slicing halfway through. The good news: it's pretty easy to see which direction the grain goes.

Slice off only as much as you'll eat (the brisket will keep better whole), and then pour some hot glaze over it and serve up some buttery polenta and roasted Brussels sprouts while you're at it.

Tomorrow, you can make a sandwich with caramelized onions, cheddar, and whole-grain mustard. The day after that you could make breakfast with some fried eggs, brisket, and collards; the day after that you can chop it up and fry it in a pan with some root vegetables and make a little hash topped with homemade hot sauce; and the day after that you'll have had the meat sweats three nights in a row, but you'll still have plenty of leftovers!

LAMB RAGU WITH CAVATELLI

This recipe predates my life with Tyler, our restaurant, and my very own birth. It's one of the biggest hits on the All Time dinner menu, and it has been soothing my soul since I was an anxious barely-adult, new to Los Angeles. Italian grandmothers have been making lamb ragu since long before I was around, which hints at the amount of skill (very little) and patience (a lot!) and soul (above all else) required to make such a comforting dish. Your house will smell like lamb for a week, but the process and the aromas, colors, and flavors are worth it because they will patch you up even if you don't think you need it. It's an emotional dish.

I took an at-home recipe that fed me for a week or longer when I was flat-broke and adapted it to a recipe that could be executed at scale by prep cooks without my hovering. Those were hard reins to drop, but surely it proves anyone can make this dish. I share it with you because it's so well-loved at All Time, and because it makes me happy to think of you falling in love with the same flavors in your own kitchen. I honestly think this dish is better suited to home cooking.

Pay attention to the details. I'm not religious, but the small things that elevate this recipe are basically just faith, attention, and time. Also, the lamb shoulder has to be bone-in. I argue with prep at work about every six months because someone starts ordering boneless shoulders. Supply chain is always the reason, but it's faster to cook boneless shoulders and a lot less work, so I'm suspicious. The bone adds flavor that you can't replicate. Truth be told, I still hover at the restaurant, and the line cooks think I'm crazy because I'm always watching and sniffing and tasting this dish compulsively during dinner service. I'm sure it's incredibly annoying for everyone.

If you lean into the long (all day or overnight) process, you'll find the dish tastes so much more satisfying. Enjoy yourself. The victory is separate from the race, and rest assured victory will come, as this dish pleases just about everyone. Except vegans.

Ragu

1 whole bone-in lamb shoulder, preferably tied in twine but this is not mandatory (just easier to handle)

Kosher salt

Equal parts chopped carrots, celery, and yellow onions—these three vegetables compose the sofrito! You should end up with 1½ to 2 cups (180 to 235 g) of each, for a total of 4½ to 5 cups (535 to 595 g) vegetables. Approximately:

2½ large carrots, washed, peeled, and diced into ¼-inch (6 mm) cubes

2½ celery stalks, washed and diced to the same shape as the carrots

2 medium yellow onions, diced like the carrots and celery

1 bottle (750 ml) Italian red wine that's decent—you wouldn't mind drinking a glass of it

Extra-virgin olive oil

1 tube (4½ ounces /130 g) double-concentrated tomato paste; I like Mutti

Leaves of 1 sprig rosemary, chopped

1 quart (960 ml) vegetable, beef, or lamb stock (NOTE: *NOT* broth, you want stock, which is not seasoned at all; you can pick this up at the butcher along with the shoulder or use just water, which is okay, too)

Filtered water

Large stockpot with tall sides

Food-handling rubber gloves really come in handy, if you can find some! *(Recipe continues)*

Pasta

....

2 cups (360 g) semolina flour, plus more for
  dusting
2 cups (250 g) type 00 flour (all-purpose works
  fine, too)
Filtered water on hand, at room temperature

To serve

....

Extra-virgin olive oil
Unsalted butter
A hunk of Parmigiano-Reggiano or Grana Padano

Make the ragu: Rinse and dry the lamb, then
generously salt it. Ideally, do this a day ahead
and let it rest in the fridge overnight on a rack
to form a slight crust; this will give you a better
sear. It will build deeper flavor, produce a better
sauce, and season the meat more fully. If you're
pressed for time, take the meat out of the fridge,
dry it, salt it, let it sit at room temperature for
30 minutes, and everything will be fine.

The meat should be tempered before searing, at
least 30 minutes or up to 1 hour, so the surface
is not too cold. Cold meat cools the oil and just
dogs your overall process for getting a nice crust.

Combine the chopped carrots, celery, and
onions (mirepoix in French, sure, but we're
Italian now, so it's sofrito) in a bowl and open
the bottle of wine; set both aside.

Coat the bottom of a tall-sided pot or Dutch
oven with olive oil and set over high heat. The
shoulder needs to be able to fit and rotate
around in there, and you want the pot deep
enough so the shoulder can get covered with
liquid and be almost entirely submerged. Once
the oil is shimmering and hot, lower the lamb
into the pan using tongs; it should sizzle loudly.
Hold the shoulder steady in place using the
tongs to get a dark, golden, crispy brown crust,
about 2 minutes, then rotate to the next surface,
2 minutes in each position. Move the meat as
little as possible and adjust the heat so it doesn't

burn. If the bits on the bottom of the pan are
getting burnt (black, bitter-smelling), lower the
heat to medium high. This process produces a
lot of smoke and takes a little patience.

Once you've gotten a nice crust on all possible
surfaces of the shoulder, lift it carefully and
place it on a resting rack. Remove any burnt
bits from the pan with a spoon. Keep the lamb
fat in the pot and lower the heat to medium.
Add the sofrito, salt it (don't go overboard), and
then reduce the heat to low. Cook slowly and
stir constantly. You can take breaks, but you
should be stirring continuously. The vegetables
will cook down until you smell not celery,
onion, and carrot as individual things, but one
singular, evocative smell that has depth. Let
it go for at least 30 to 45 minutes. Longer is
better on this step; don't skimp.

Raise the heat to medium high and add the
entire tube of tomato paste and continue
stirring constantly. After about 10 minutes, the
paste will become a deep, rusty color and the
smell will be sweeter and more fragrant than
the plain tomato scent from the tube.

Stir the chopped rosemary into the sofrito.
Increase the heat to high and add the wine. Let
the alcohol cook off over high heat for about
8 minutes and then return the lamb shoulder
to the pot. Add the stock and filtered water,
submerging three-quarters of the lamb in
liquid, so it's barely exposed.

Bring everything to a boil, then turn the heat
down low so you're on a bare simmer, cover
with a lid, and cook for at least 4 hours. At
2 hours, check the liquid levels; if you need
to, add more filtered water to keep three-
quarters of the shoulder submerged (a little
less is okay). At 4 hours, check the meat with a
fork. Sometimes I can grab and pull the blade
bone if it's accessible, to see if it's loose. It's
ready when the meat effortlessly falls off the
bone. Go longer if it's not. I've had shoulders
take as long as 8 hours. You   *(Recipe continues)*

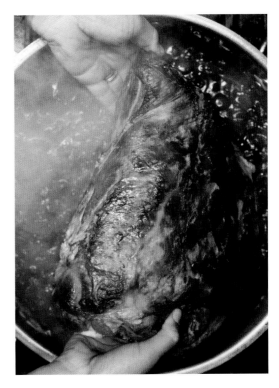

The Cook Book of All Time   93

can't really overcook it, but you don't want to be under. I prefer to braise on the stovetop, but you can put the whole pot, covered, in a preheated 250°F (120°C) oven for about 6 hours. Check the liquid level every hour and keep the shoulder about 75 percent submerged, adding water or stock as needed.

When the shoulder blade is totally loose and you can pull it right out, it's done. Turn the heat off and keep the meat in the braising liquid. Let the lamb cool in the liquid for 1 hour.

Once cooled (you should be able to touch the liquid), use tongs to pull the meat out and place onto a baking sheet or resting rack. Remove the bone (it should slide right out), find some rubber gloves, and then begin pulling the meat. This part is super messy. Separating the meat from fat, skin, tendon, and bone takes a long time and is tedious, but extremely important. I recommend gloves because the meat will still be hot, and you'll avoid having the scent of lamb on your hands for a week. The more work you put in here, the better it will be. Once you have a pile of picked meat, without any tendon or coarse fat bits, run a chef's knife through it all for a coarse chop.

Strain the liquid from the pot through a fine-mesh strainer, or a colander, over another large pot. This step isn't mandatory, it'll just yield a glossier, more refined sauce. Sometimes we skip it at the restaurant, and that's when a bit of rosemary or visible carrot ends up in the sauce (which I love), just a bit more rustic. Skip straining if you put the empty milk carton back in the fridge; do it if you make your bed every day.

Put the lamb back in the sauce (strained or not), and bring it up to a gentle boil, then lower the heat and reduce it uncovered. Salt to taste as you go. You're going for a glossy, deep, thicker-than-water but thinner-than-ranch-dressing sauce. It should be thick enough to coat the back of a spoon but still slide off,

probably 45 minutes to 1 hour of cooking, depending on the liquid you have left.

Make the pasta: I like to make the pasta the same day as the lamb, while the braise is going.

Mix the flours together on a nice clean, smooth work surface. Make a mountain shape out of the flour mixture, and then turn it into a volcano by making a well at the peak, the size of a golf ball, let's say. Pour a small amount of lukewarm filtered water to fill the well, and swirl it around with your fingers to incorporate into the flour. Repeat this process until your flour is a dough and you have a flaky ball to work with. Not too wet. Then add a small amount of water and knead it with the palm of your hand until the water becomes totally incorporated. This is physical labor—be prepared to work your arms. Press down through your palm and keep folding the dough in on itself, until it is springy and smooth. Let the dough rest for at least 30 minutes, wrapped in plastic wrap in the fridge.

Roll or press out the dough so that you have a slab about ½ inch (12 mm) thick. The shape doesn't matter too much. From the slab of dough, cut strips ½ inch (12 mm) wide and roll those into ropes. The ropes can be any length and should be about ¼ inch (6 mm) thick. To make the pasta, the fastest way would be to order a Fante's Cousin Elisa's Cavatelli Maker on the internet for less than fifty dollars (a hand-cranking, very analog, very cheap piece of equipment). You attach it to the counter and then feed the long ropes through and little pastas fly out the other end, shaped and ready. This specialty contraption is likely to break after two to four uses, so if you'd like to go the totally handmade route, cut the ropes into 2-inch (5 cm) segments. Drag your fingertips or the end of a butter knife across the pieces, one at a time. Press down and pull toward you; the dough should be springy enough to handle this. You'll get sort of canoe-shaped pastas, *(Recipe continues)*

around 1 to 1½ inches (2.5 to 4 cm) long. This shape is totally suitable for this sauce!

Once your pasta is made, spread them out on a baking sheet sprinkled with semolina—do not layer your pasta! I've seen line cooks carry three sheet trays stacked, as if to save time, only to yield a giant glob of dough and a lot of wasted time, flour, and water. Don't do that. You can freeze pasta for later use—they actually cook wonderfully from frozen. Just coat them with semolina and store in a plastic bag in individual portions—1 cup (240 ml) by volume per bag. To cook from frozen, toss them into salted boiling water and pull them out with a mesh strainer once they float to the top, about 3 minutes. If you're cooking pasta from its fresh state, blanch them in salted boiling water till they float to the top (less than 1 minute), then pull out with a mesh strainer and place onto a sheet pan and set aside.

To serve: Toss the blanched pasta into a hot sauté pan with some olive oil and maybe a little butter to warm and crisp them up a bit, and when you feel they're looking good, after about 45 seconds, add a ladle of the ragu. Let it combine. Everything is fully cooked at this point, so you're just incorporating it and bringing it to hot serving temperature; it should take less than 5 minutes if the ragu is just off the heat. Plate it and finish with shaved Parm, using a peeler, and a bit more olive oil.

Polenta, dried rigatoni, and even just good toasted bread also make smart conduits for ragu. Some purists don't even add Parm; I definitely do. Personally, I find red pepper flakes offensive in this context and absolutely hate it when people ask for them for this dish at All Time. But I'm not at your house and you're in charge.

You can jar the remaining ragu and refrigerate it for up to 1 week. If you do this, top the jar with olive oil so there's no air between the lid and the ragu. When reheating, get a pan hot with a little olive oil in it and add 1 cup (240 ml) of the cold ragu. Let it heat and then add a little bit of butter to bring it together. That's kind of cheating, some Italians would say, but it's also kind of delicious and everyone gets to pick and choose which rules they violate and how they justify it. Prepare pasta (or bread or an empty bowl and a spoon) per instructions.

PIQUE HOT SAUCE

Pique sauce embodies everything I find romantic about cooking—it's rooted in tradition but so personal and differs from place to place. It's a vinegar-based hot sauce, and below is a simple base recipe that's great as is but allows for some improv and personal expression. What's most exciting is that it works on almost everything—crispy rice, fried eggs, beans, as a marinade for chicken or pork, any taco imaginable, and my favorite use, glazing roasted vegetables. The applications are infinite. You can even mix the pique with some crème fraîche or Greek yogurt to make an erotic dipping sauce for all kinds of things.

The impact of ingredients will change a bit with the seasons—chiles are hotter in the fall, carrots get sweeter in the winter—so be sure to taste and adjust.

Makes about 1 quart (1 L)

2 carrots, peeled and sliced about ½ inch (12 mm) thick
1 white onion, diced into ½ inch (12 mm) cubes
4 chiles de árbol or similar dried chiles
1 garlic clove
1 tablespoon kosher salt
2½ cups (600 ml) filtered water
2 cups (480 ml) white vinegar
1 serrano chile, sliced in half the long way with the stem intact

Place the carrots, onion, dried chiles, garlic clove, salt, and water in a medium saucepan. Cook over medium heat for 10 to 12 minutes; the carrots should be tender enough to mash with a fork. Let cool for a few minutes.

Pour the mixture into a blender or use an immersion blender to blend it until it's totally pureed, 45 to 60 seconds. Pour into a bottle or jar and add the vinegar and serrano. Give it a mix or a shake, and a taste for seasoning and spice. The flavors will intensify as the sauce sits so don't go nuts with the spice. It will last a long time in the refrigerator. I've been known to just top ours up with a little more vinegar when it gets low.

THE ORIGINAL RED HOT SAUCE OF ALL TIME

This was the first hot sauce we had, and it's a project that began when we opened in 2018. Since then, nearly everyone who's come through our kitchen has contributed to the recipe. Our hats are off to the proverbial village, past and present, for raising this wild child. We put it on breakfast burritos, crispy rice, tacos, and pork, and we get requests for it all day and night—even at dinnertime when we don't really serve it. It can go on everything. It's spicy but still keeps tons of flavor, thanks to a good amount of acid and the way the chiles impart sweetness and punch.

Do keep in mind that blending chiles is how pepper spray is made, so be careful not to breathe it in, and mind what you touch after handling chiles. Gloves are an option. Ventilation is key. So is not touching your eyeballs or your anything else balls, okay?

Makes about 2 cups (480 ml)

1 habanero chile, stem removed
8 ounces (225 g) fresno chiles, stems removed
2 cloves garlic, peeled
1 cup (240 ml) white vinegar
1 cup (240 ml) apple cider vinegar
½ cup (120 ml) filtered water
Kosher salt

Place the habanero, fresnos, garlic, vinegars, and water in a heavy-bottomed saucepan or Dutch oven. Bring to a boil, then reduce the heat to a simmer. Simmer for 1 hour, uncovered. Let it cool for about 30 minutes.

Add to a blender and puree, or blend with an immersion blender until smooth. Salt to taste. Store it in a jar or portion into cute little bottles. Hot sauce lasts in the refrigerator for at least 1 month.

DAYTIME CRISPY RICE

We get a lot of requests for this recipe. People say to me, "I tried to make it at home and it's just not the same!" I hear that a lot. I always think to myself, *Well, yeah, no shit. We have a whole restaurant.* Here's the tip: Rice that's too hydrated won't get crispy no matter what you do. Rice really needs to dry out. Then you can make it sing. Here's how to do it right:

1½ tablespoons extra-virgin olive oil
¼ red onion, thinly sliced
2 cups (400 g) cooked short-grain rice, like sushi or arborio (see page 34)
1½ cups (135 g) broccoli or Broccolini florets, cut into smaller pieces, 1½ inches (4 cm) long for cooking. Vegetable options also include bok choy, carrots, snap peas, kale, or pea tendrils; get excited and make it your own. Use about ¾ cup of each additional vegetable, which will make a lot more food but leftovers on this one are as good or better.
Kosher salt
2 tablespoons tamari or soy sauce, plus more as needed
Juice of 1 lemon, plus more as needed
Fried eggs (optional)
Pique Hot Sauce (optional; page 100)

This recipe moves quickly. You'll need two—yes, two—8- or 10-inch (20 or 25 cm) cast-iron or carbon steel pans, plus tongs and a spatula. You'll be cooking in both pans at the same time, so ready all of your necessary tools and ingredients to feel organized.

Get both pans ready on the burner and turn the heat up to high on one pan for about 45 seconds. Add the olive oil and heat until it shimmers, about 1 minute.

Add the onion to the hot pan, give it a stir, and let it cook for another 45 seconds. We're looking for the edges to start browning nicely. Add the rice, stir it up a little bit, and gently work it into an even layer in the bottom of the pan. Turn the heat down to medium high and let the rice cook, undisturbed, for 2 minutes. While the rice and onions are crispifying, turn the heat to high on the second pan and heat the olive oil for 1 minute, then add the vegetables of your choosing to this pan. They'll cook up a little before being added to the rice and release their water, so it doesn't go into the rice you're working so hard to get crisp (the key is dry, remember!). Salt the vegetables and toss, taking maybe 1 or 2 minutes to cook them, depending on what you're using. When the vegetables are tender but not mush, turn off the heat. The rice should be making some sounds and scents that signal all things crispy and delicious. You know the ones. I haven't been to your house (yet), so I don't know your stove. Trust your senses; if it's not crispy and toasty-smelling, give the rice another minute.

Once you've unlocked the crispiness, add the cooked vegetables to the pan with the rice and incorporate them together. Use the spatula if anything is sticking. Ideally, some of the rice that hasn't crisped up will land on the bottom of the pan, getting its due chance. Let it cook another 2 minutes. The vegetables should be tender but still have some bite. It's important not to over stir, as there are starches in the rice that will start to work out and then we're making a recipe called Weird Gummy Rice.

Add the tamari and lemon juice. It should sizzle and smell even more delicious. Give it a little stir so everything gets sauced. Taste for seasoning, adding more tamari and squeezing in another lemon, if needed. *(Recipe continues)*

Pile it into a bowl, onto a plate, or eat it out of the pan. We top it with fried eggs and pique sauce at the restaurant. Avocado, salmon, bacon, steak, and pork shoulder have all been done to great acclaim. And just like that, once you get your first phony workers' comp lawsuit, you now qualify as a restaurant owner, too.

STREET CORN SALAD

Corn defines summer for me. This dish makes me feel like a carefree child. The treasured moments of summer from my youth are ever fleeting, and this dish is an hour of childhood, if you ask me. If you don't agree or don't like summer somehow, well, it's still damn fine corn. As this is a book of suggestions, far be it from me to tell you what to do, just don't you dare make this with commodity corn. There's no point. Have a bowl of spiced mayonnaise instead. Making this corn is a moment in time and one to be honored. I have a vivid memory of Ashley sitting on a milk crate shucking corn in the backyard the week we started dating. That image will stay with me forever. When I stumble upon the memory, it's like finding an old picture of your parents, one that transports you to a time and a place you can feel even if you weren't there. Well, I was there and it's a special scene.

Suffice it to say you'll need some. Corn, that is. Good corn. Hopefully from a farmer not too far away. Or a reputable corn-selling outfit, at minimum.

Serves 4

6 ears good corn, shucked
3 tablespoons quality mayonnaise (we use Kewpie)
Juice of 2 limes
1½ tablespoons kosher salt
3 ounces (85 g) queso cotija
2 teaspoons smoked paprika, or cayenne if you
   like more spice
¼ bunch cilantro, leaves picked

On a grill or over the stove burners, lay the corn over the flame until it gets a-poppin' and turns brown with blackened edges. Rotate it every minute or so until it's 70 percent grilled. If you use high-quality corn, it's delicious both cooked and uncooked so the mix adds some variety to the finished product.

Get the widest bowl you have. Find a round container with a flat bottom, like an empty yogurt container or something regrettably made of plastic. A pint deli is what we use, but you're unlikely to know what that is, and less likely to have one. Imagine an empty ice cream pint but durable. Find the closest approximation to that, turn it upside down, and set it in the bottom of the bowl. Balance an ear of corn point side down on the bottom of the yogurt container or what have you and slice the kernels off the cob from the top down, then repeat with the rest of the corn. The yogurt cup prevents you from bashing your knife into the side of the bowl, which would be unpleasant and knife-dulling, not to mention dangerous-ish. If you don't have anything that'll work, just be a little more cautious as you slice the kernels into the bowl. Or less reckless anyway.

Add the mayonnaise, lime juice, and salt. Toss or mix with a big spoon and have a taste. Pile it up in your favorite corn vessel and top it with grated cotija and smoked paprika, then decorate it with cilantro leaves. Burn this book and take credit for inventing this recipe.

THE SALMON BOWL

"Boy, everyone wants to know how to make the Salmon Bowl. In a book filled with hopefully simple food, the thought of writing this recipe scares me, let alone making it from scratch at home for one meal. This should be the last recipe in the book so it hopefully gets edited out because it's going to be eight pages."

—**Tyler, guy who can do electrical work, make a twelve-foot table in four hours, and invent a cheesecake recipe on the fly**

Tyler insists that this recipe is too complicated and "scary" and not doable for home cooks (direct quote: "it hopefully gets edited out"). Never mind that he doesn't like salmon and never eats this; Chef Paul has the thing for lunch every day, so he's sick of it and wants to change it and won't talk to me about it much. And YET: Every day people come for lunch and fawn over the Salmon Bowl and sing its praises. I also happen to love it and eat it almost daily. Both delicious and virtuous, I maintain it's also very *choose your expletive* easy to make, and though I don't have to because I own a restaurant, I urge you to prove Tyler wrong. You basically need to cook rice, cook salmon, make a simple dressing, and cut some cabbage and avocado. You can go off-script and substitute broccoli for the cabbage, and you can add a fried egg. It's not that hard. For a restaurant that has four rice recipes, took two years to figure out chocolate chip cookies, and makes its own bread for the entire menu, this dish is the least of anyone's worries. If you love it, or think you'll love it, even better because you'll be set up to have some extra of each item to eat for lunch a few days during the week, or be the hero and make it for some friends on strip poker night. It's a healthy dish that's perfect for a weeknight dinner or lunch and everyone should give it credit, because if you took a poll, the lunch line at All Time would be 75 percent Salmon Bowl orders.

Slaw

....

½ head red cabbage, thinly sliced
1 serrano chile, thinly sliced
Fresh cilantro leaves
Juice of 1 lemon
¼ teaspoon good-quality sesame oil

Rice

....

Warm sushi rice (Rice in the Oven, page 35, works perfectly)

Lemon-Soy Dressing

....

1 tablespoon sugar
½ cup (120 ml) soy sauce or tamari
Zest of 1 lemon
¼ cup (60 ml) fresh-squeezed lemon juice
½ cup (120 ml) filtered water
¼ cup (60 ml) rice vinegar
1 tablespoon shichimi togarashi (Japanese spice mixture)

Cucumber

....

1 cucumber, cut into chunks
1 cup (240 ml) rice vinegar (for pickling)
1 tablespoon kosher salt (for pickling)
1 tablespoon sugar (for pickling; optional)

Salmon

....

One 5- to 6-ounce (140 to 170 g) skin-on salmon fillet
Kosher salt
Freshly ground black pepper (optional)
Extra-virgin olive oil

(Recipe continues)

Serving

....

½ avocado
Sesame seeds
Furikake (traditional Japanese rice seasoning
    containing sesame seeds and seaweed)
Fried or hard-boiled egg (optional)
Sichimi togarashi (optional)

Make the slaw: Put the cabbage, serrano, cilantro leaves, lemon juice, and sesame oil in a large bowl. Toss it all together and set aside. Wow. So hard. Moving on.

Make the rice, per page 35. Perhaps you even have some already made in your fridge, ready to go. Great. Again, moving on.

Make the lemon-soy dressing: Put the sugar in a medium bowl first. Then add the rest of the ingredients and give it a vigorous whisking. Yeah, that's it. You'll have dressing to spare. Store it in the fridge and it'll keep 1 week.

Make the cucumber: If you want to make pickles, place the chunks of cucumber in a medium bowl with the rice vinegar, salt, and, if using, sugar. You can quick-pickle for now, but if you want extra for another day (true pickles), just use more than one cucumber. If you don't feel like pickling, the cucumber chunks will be delicious with the dressing. We'll call them raw pickles.

Make the salmon: Preheat the oven to 400°F (200°C).

Pat dry and salt your portion of salmon. Add pepper if you like. Get an ovenproof sauté pan on medium high with some olive oil in it. When it's hot, lay the salmon skin side down in the pan, away from you so it doesn't splatter at your face. Let it cook for about 4 minutes, and then, as Tyler likes to say, whack it in the oven for another 5 to 8 minutes, depending on how you like your salmon. In this approach you're getting

crispy skin and a roasty top on this fillet, and that's what's nice about the pan to oven method. You can also just do one or the other. If you're just roasting, expect about 8 to 12 minutes. If you're just using the pan, 4 minutes per side.

If you're a meal-prepping kind of cook, you can also roast a larger portion of salmon in the oven, like a whole side or several 5- to 6-ounce (140 to 170 g) portions. Then you can take some from the fridge for a bowl when you want a nice lunch without cooking. To do that, season the side of salmon (or several portions) with salt (and pepper if you're into it), and roast on a baking sheet at 400°F (205°C) until done, about 15 minutes.

To serve: Put your rice in a bowl; if you have an ice cream scoop use that so it'll look nice and profesh, like you're at All Time, except you won't have to wait in line for the bathroom. Next to that, put a handful of slaw. Now add the half avocado and the cucumbers. Lay the cooked salmon fillet on top, with artistry. Keep words like "adorn" and "atop" to yourself. If you're going to add a fried egg, you should have done that by now. Boiled works, too, and maybe you have one on hand. Now's the time to sprinkle it all with sesame seeds and furikake, perhaps a little togarashi. Spoon the dressing over any part of the bowl or the whole thing, wherever and however you want. Eat it and call the restaurant to let us know which one of us won the recipe-off. The conclusion is that you have, because you can now make a salmon bowl on demand, which, according to Tyler's logic, is basically nuclear fission. And it only took a few paragraphs!

CRUNCHY NUT SALSA

I almost certainly didn't invent this so-called nut salsa, but also this recipe isn't based on anything I've ever had so who knows where it started. Not important. We don't use it much at All Time, as nuts present a high degree of danger, but privately we like to put these nuts on everything, and that should inspire not only a dirty joke but also a tasty home-cooked meal because it's so easy.

One morning I woke up thinking about dinner. That happens to guys like me. Fish with some crunchy, nutty, spicy, herbaceous condiment topper felt like the right answer. It was an uncomfortably hot day and we were having dinner at an antique (falling down) old Hollywood mansion where some friends were house-sitting. I offered to come over and cook dinner so we could get a free swim and cool off a bit in a pool that was last serviced fifty years prior; the diving board's caution tape must have blown away because it was . . . not safe-looking. The front end was touching the water, like the ghost of a very heavy figure was standing on it. That and the rusty springs were enough to ward off a novice diver like myself. We were lucky there was water to swim in at all.

Anyway, I try not to cook inside in the summer unless I'm making Ashley's birthday cake, so we made a meal for six on a Weber grill after our swim. Fish, vegetables, more vegetables, probably some tortillas, too. I don't really remember other than that was the night nut salsa was born. At least ours was. This stuff was the star of the evening. I asked around and no one remembers whether we ate sea bass or shoe leather, but you bet your Ts and As we all remember the salsa.

Here's how it got made:

Makes 1 cup (240 ml)

1 dried smoked chile, a chipotle or chile de árbol preferred; if you use a guajillo or pasilla or mild dried chiles, add half a diced jalapeño for some heat
1 cup (120 g) Marcona almonds
Stems from 1 bunch cilantro, chopped as small as you can, leaves reserved for garnish
1 teaspoon flaky sea salt
Drizzle of good extra-virgin olive oil
Juice of 2 to 3 limes

If you have a mortar and pestle, now is the time to use it. If not, it's only a little more work. If using a mortar and pestle, crush up the dried chile first, then add the nuts and crush those. Go slow, it'll be better. Don't make almond butter; the nuts should still have dimension, like little pebbles or slightly smaller.

You can also just chop the Marconas and chop up the dried chile. It'll be dry and brittle and kind of a hassle but worth it.

Once the dried chile and nuts are combined, add the cilantro stems. If you're using fresh jalapeño, add that now. Then add the salt.

Add the olive oil and lime juice last, 5 minutes before serving. Mix it all together with a spoon and let it stand for another minute or two so the chile hydrates a little.

Taste for heat and salt level, and adjust if needed. Spice will intensify a little bit as it sits but not too much.

Put it on grilled fish, roasted vegetables, steaks, tacos—just about anything. It'll keep in the fridge, in a sealed container, for 3 to 4 days.

GUACAMOLE

This feels like such a silly recipe to write unless you think about all the guacamole you've had. I used to work in a four-star hotel where the guacamole was just avocado puree from a plastic bag we'd mix with Pace salsa. I think it was a four-star hotel. Anyway, I'm sure the shrimp I had to defrost every night were top-quality free-range.

I don't have too many proprietary secrets but I do make dang good guacamole, and it has been on the table for 98 percent of our summertime dinners and finds its way onto the All Time menu next to pork shoulder and tortillas, also usually in the summer. It deserves to be more than an afterthought. If you want to try it, start here and adjust to your preferences along the way.

Makes 2 to 3 cups (480 to 720 ml)

3 good tomatoes like Romas or Early Girls, or even on-the-vine tomatoes from a good grocery store (or 1 cup [145 g] cherry tomatoes, about 15, halved)
½ red onion, very finely diced
1 jalapeño or serrano chile with the stem and seeds, very finely diced
¼ bunch cilantro leaves, finely chopped, plus more to taste
Juice of 3 limes, plus more to taste
2 teaspoons kosher salt, plus more to taste
3 ripe avocados
1 pack corn tortillas and fancy salt, if you're making chips

First, we need to make some really great pico de gallo. Nothing fancy. And here's a key to the whole thing: If you're using large tomatoes, quarter them through the stem end and scoop out all the seeds and insides. This way, you won't water it down. Press the slices flat and

dice them into about ¼-inch (6 mm) squares. If you're using cherry tomatoes, don't bother removing the insides; halving them is enough work. Add to a large mixing bowl along with the diced onion, jalapeño, cilantro, half the lime juice, and half the salt.

Mix it up and taste it. It should pack a punch of acidity, spice, onion, and salt. If not, adjust to your taste with salt, lime, and cilantro.

Once you have a pico that tastes a little too great, meaning a little too spicy and the acidity makes you take a knee, set it aside.

Pit, peel, and dice the avocados. There are a few ways to do this. Once halved and pitted, I slice them in the skin to make cubes and scoop them out with a spoon, but that can be a little, um, dicey since you're cutting into the palm of your hand. You can scoop the halves out intact with a spoon and dice them on a cutting board, or you can lazily scoop out pieces with a spoon. Set aside.

Now make the chips! Quarter your corn tortillas so you have triangles (assuming your tortillas are round). Cut as many as you dare to eat. Pour about ½ inch of olive oil into a large cast-iron pan and set it over medium-high heat. After about 3 minutes, the olive oil should be hot (350°F/175°C). Scatter the cut tortillas into the oil in a single layer. They'll bubble and crisp up in about 90 seconds or less; flip them with tongs or a fish spatula and go another minute. Pull them from the oil onto paper towels or a resting rack. Salt them with the fancy salt and set aside. Don't make too many extra because they are so delicious that your wife will likely crunch them in bed well after 10 p.m. while you're trying to sleep, and you'll wake up with corn chip indentations on your face or worse. *(Recipe continues)*

Gently add the avocado to the pico. Use a big spoon and fold everything together. The avocado should retain texture and shape while joining all its friends to make a sum that is greater than its parts. Think of the end goal as being more an avocado salsa than guacamole, if that helps you keep from turning it into a puree for babies.

Taste it. Use a chip! Maybe some more salt? Lime juice, perhaps? You are the captain now. You can always mix it more to find the texture you like for scooping and such, but good luck going the other way. Less is more.

SWEET TOOTH

A Quick Note on Baking

You'd never believe it, but I don't enjoy taking directions just for the sake of it. School fell apart for me in the third grade because I wasn't such a follow-directions sort of kid then, either. Recipes are generally not great at providing context so that you can understand what's happening. And that's how you learn and how you become confident cooking. I mostly see recipes that tell you the next step and then the next, using the most outlandish verbs and assuming you innately know the difference between soft peaks and stiff peaks. You're just walking blindfolded with your arms out hoping you get to the right place. I find them unnecessarily complex and rarely learn anything from just following steps.

Baking recipes can be the peak offenders of *how* rather than *why*. My goal here is to illuminate a little why, demonstrate a little how, and slap you on the ass so you can get out there and enjoy separating the wet ingredients from the dry ones, instead of just mixing them all together. Because you *understand* what's going on, and you can adapt; if you have the *why* in your back pocket you can tackle most anything you want to cook.

Per the list at the beginning of this very book, you need to get a digital scale. And, as stated, *use* the digital scale, especially when it comes to baking. A cup of flour will be two different weights five times in a row. Or in Ashley's case, every time you make pie dough. Once you do get in the habit of using a scale, you'll never go back.

BETSY'S COBBLER

I grew up in West Virginia. We lived at the intersection of rural nature and mountain culture. Our little town hosted an internationally known folk music workshop and festival in the summer that probably has cultural significance, but I only remember losing my whole carnival budget trying to win a 6 x 6-inch reflective Skid Row mirror. I did not win the item.

I was lucky to grow up where people could live a traditional life if they liked, whatever that meant to them. To us, it meant spending summers on Chuck and Bridget's mountain, family friends who lived a true mountain existence. Chuck was a traditional Appalachian woodworker who could build anything and do it without power tools. I spent my childhood there, learning to camp, hiking, going to barn dances where my dad's Dixieland band, the Appal Core, played, and also, picking blackberries.

In summer we'd head out to the meadows with our buckets and fill them with wild blackberries. Our fingers would be stained black and full of prickers. We'd eat a lot of our haul during the pick, lengthening the process. Then my mom would make cobbler. She only made it once or twice a year, but it's ever-present in memory. It had its own folklore, the way things do when you're a kid. You don't question something like cobbler, you enjoy it because your mom made it. I lived twenty-five years before I ever even considered attempting to make one myself.

I had just assumed it was nearly impossible to make and that's why it only materialized once or twice a year. We drove to a friend's mountain to pick wild blackberries just to make it. The cobbler is so dear to me. It represents the pinnacle of summer but also something more.

I lost my mom in my late twenties. I didn't do any therapy other than eating a lot of Long John Silver's and riding my bike. I'll skip over that part, it's too private and too big, but ultimately, I did find myself ready to attempt her cobbler recipe.

We put the cobbler on the All Time menu as dessert, even though in my home we ate it for breakfast. It became an homage to her on top of all that it already was. It's so deeply personal that I still hover over the prep cooks and adjust the most meaningless parts of the procedure to cling to its origin and keep it "mine."

It's never come off the dessert menu and has become a much-loved item, and I'm grateful for that because it was a big risk to put it out there to the public. Thankfully people generally love it as much as I do, but there was an *LA Times* food critic who suggested that our family recipe would be more accurately called a "buckle," and he was just flat-out wrong and narrowly escaped having his own belt stuffed up his ass, hardware first. No offense.

One night, we had a very high-profile guest at the restaurant. I'm not one to name names, but it was a big deal for the West Virginian in me, who still thinks this sort of thing is very cool. This movie star, whom you would never expect to see in real life, came in with two friends and the three of them had dessert for five, which included two cobblers so that the aforementioned could have one all to himself. That in itself was amazing, and I'm sitting next to him and thinking, yes, he is quite cool and indeed very handsome in real life, although he could never buy a better air conditioner than the one we have—he could get an equal one, but not better.

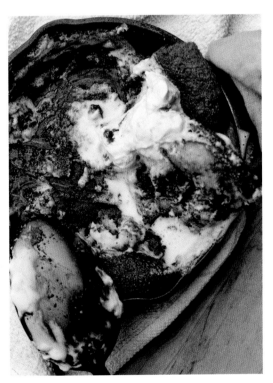

So the day after this Hollywood so-and-so came in and polished off his cobbler right in front of me, I go into the prep kitchen and begin to make an impassioned, lengthy speech in Spanish; I've been taking a class every morning for two years that culminates in a monologue to Elvira, our wonderful prep cook who's been with us for years.

Anyway, I'm so desperate to convey to her how this recipe is the most tangible thing I have of my mom's legacy, and this A-lister who I think is cool loved it so much he had to have his own! I'm going on and on about how this means so much, because it is so much more than just some flour and butter baked up into an item; I'm telling her how humbled I am that she puts so much love and care into the cobbler—like I do or like my mom did—that it even turns out better than when I make it! I'm trying to express how grateful I am because this dish is just so important to me and our family and how she's part of this family and after about six minutes of attempting to convey all of this in terrible Spanish until I'm blue in the face, I pause for a second. Elvira just looks at me and politely says, "The dishwasher made it."

Elvira herself went from introverted dishwasher to the linchpin of our prep operation, and she also has a subtle kind of wit I haven't yet fully pinpointed. I'll never know if she was just being gracious, trying not to take credit, or making a joke. But the point is, it's very easy to make and stupefyingly delicious. It's a thing that makes me feel the good kind of nostalgia, the kind that might not kill me. The ease of making it in no way corresponds to its specialness or crowd-pleasingness, or personal significance.

BETSY'S COBBLER WITH WHIPPED CRÈME FRAICHE

This is a great base recipe. It's really simple and you can develop a personal taste for how you like to make it; you can use various kinds of

fruit, both fresh and frozen. You might use less sugar for riper fruit or more sugar for tart fruit, or vanilla instead of almond extract (though for me almond is key). You can dazzle movie stars. You can substitute some sour cream or yogurt for half of the milk, if you like the tang. If it's summer and you're using peaches instead of berries, I'd do half milk, half sour cream, and that would be one hell of a buckle, whatever the hell a gd buckle is.

In accordance with tradition, I always use cups instead of grams for this one. That's how my mom wrote it down, and that's how we do it at home still. Metrics are provided because I already lectured you on scaling baking ingredients and perhaps you're living outside the confines of the imperial system, so you can do either as I say or as I do, in this case only.

Cobbler

....

1 cup (125 g) all-purpose flour
¾ cup (150 g) granulated sugar
2 teaspoons baking powder
1 teaspoon kosher salt
¾ cup (180 ml) whole milk
4 tablespoons (½ stick/55 g) unsalted butter, plus extra for greasing the pan
2 cups fruit, such as berries, sliced peaches, and nectarines, pitted cherries . . . your choice!
¼ teaspoon almond extract
2 tablespoons confectioners' sugar
Flaky sea salt

Whipped Crème Fraîche (or vanilla ice cream)

....

½ cup (120 ml) crème fraîche
½ cup (120 ml) heavy cream
2 tablespoons confectioners' sugar

Preheat the oven to 350°F (175°F).

Make the cobbler: Mix the flour, sugar, baking powder, and salt in a large bowl. Add the milk and stir with a rubber spatula. Mix until just incorporated and still a little lumpy. Melt the butter and set aside.

Butter an 8-inch (20 cm) cast-iron skillet. A glass cake pan or baking dish can also work.

Toss the fruit, almond extract, and confectioners' sugar together in a medium bowl. Confectioners' sugar has some cornstarch in it so when the fruit starts to release water as it cooks, the powdered sugar will help coax out a nice sauce.

Scrape the batter into the skillet and then spread the fruit mix over the top.

Pour the melted butter over the whole thing and bake until it's deep brown, smells like heaven, and the center is set, 40 to 45 minutes.

Make the whipped crème fraîche: Combine the crème fraîche and heavy cream in a large bowl. Add the confectioners' sugar and whisk until nice peaks form (by hand or use a mixer on medium-high speed). Don't overmix, you'll end up with butter! The peaks should stand up on their own and the mixture should stay mostly in the bowl if you flip it upside down.

Once the cobbler is done, let it cool for 20 minutes. When ready to serve, top the cobbler with the whipped crème fraîche, a little flaky salt, and eat it. Or do a scoop of store-bought vanilla ice cream. It's actually more traditional to serve it this way, but we don't have a freezer at All Time and my wife prefers whip!

Once you have a stomachache, just leave the remaining cobbler on the stove loosely covered with foil and a spoon on top (to secure the foil) for a day or two. When you walk by, take a bite but leave the spoon. That's how we did it growing up.

SCONES

I used to have a fantasy that I'd retire to the mountains of North Carolina, grow some food, and live a simple life in the woods. I shared this with a close friend many years back and he said, "Yeah, but then you'd start thinking about how there's no good goat cheese around so you'd buy some goats and end up being a full-time goat rancher." Joke's on him because, while I do love goat cheese, I've already found a simple life, owning and running a restaurant that's open seventeen hours a day, every day. And anyway, where we live there's plenty of goat cheese but not a lot of good scones. I'm wired to make things better that aren't good but could easily be really, really good. Our whole restaurant is based on this notion, on the idea of simple things done well. And in principle, a sweet, crumbly breakfast-y flour-sugar-butter situation should be delicious. Now obviously I haven't had every scone in America, just most of them. This recipe will procure you the best of the best. I'm a real scone pusher when people are eyeing our baked goods. They look at me suspiciously. I get it. The pastry-consuming public has been burned too many times: bad, dry scones that somehow taste old even fresh out of the oven. However, I stand by my scone skeptic-to-lover conversion rate (SSTLCR) of 100 percent and I'll challenge you to prove me wrong.

500 grams (4 cups) all-purpose flour, plus more as needed
110 grams (½ cup plus 1 tablespoon) granulated sugar
2 tablespoons baking powder
1 teaspoon kosher salt
395 grams (1¾ cups) frozen unsalted butter, grated or cut into small cubes
175 grams (1¼ cups) blackberries and/or raspberries
1 teaspoon lemon zest
360 milliliters heavy cream, plus more as needed for dipping

120 grams sour cream
Turbinado sugar, like Sugar in the Raw, also for dipping

Preheat the oven to 375°F (190°C).

Mix the flour, sugar, baking powder, and kosher salt in a large bowl. Cut in the butter and massage with your hands or use a pastry cutter—you know, that weird brass-knuckle-looking tool that everyone has but never uses. The proper incorporation of chilled butter is what makes anything flaky—scones, biscuits, pie dough, croissants. It's not a hard task, but it is a specific one. Chunks of butter that are too large will melt in the oven and make a greasy mess, and butter that's too soft won't incorporate properly and will turn your dough into batter, which will get weird. Let's not make it weird. As I said, it's important to keep the butter cold so it doesn't melt. You can also grate it frozen directly into the bowl of dry ingredients. We're looking to incorporate pea-size pieces of butter into the flour so it's crumbly.

Add the berries and lemon zest to the bowl and incorporate with your hands. The berries should be evenly distributed.

Add the heavy cream and sour cream and mix with a wooden spoon until all the liquid is picked up by the dry ingredients, about 30 seconds. It will be heavy and hard to mix. The dough should be wet and shaggy, and there shouldn't be any liquid sitting in the bottom of the bowl. You might find it easier to mix with your hands.

If it's truly too wet to work with, you can sprinkle a little flour over the top. If it feels really dry and couldn't possibly hold the shape of a loose ball, incorporate a little more cream. *(Recipe continues)*

Pull a heaping half cup of dough out of the bowl. They make ice cream scoops in ounce sizes, and a ½ cup is 4 ounces (120 ml), so if you have one of those, that's a nice tool for the job at hand. The dough should hold together loosely and weigh around 150 grams. Gently form it into a ball like you would a snowball and place on a baking sheet. You can freeze scones beautifully at this point for about a month, and you can bake them straight from frozen and they'll come out perfect. If you're freezing, they can be placed close together on a tray or in large plastic bags, arranged in rows. When baking from frozen, plan to bake longer, 20 to 25 minutes.

If you're baking them now, dip the scones in some heavy cream and then dip them into raw sugar. Return them to the baking sheet with ample room between each. We bake six per full-size baking sheet; they will spread out quite a lot because of the butter. Bake for 15 to 20 minutes, until beautifully browned. As always, know your oven and use your senses, and also a cake tester, thermometer, or the tip of a small knife so you can poke the middle when the scones are nice and golden brown. When the knife comes out clean, take the scones out of the oven to cool for 10 to 15 minutes. Eat them fresh, hand them out, become a hero.

PIE DOUGH

It's early, but I'm awake. Still in bed—the vacant sheets and undisturbed comforter next to me feel expansive. I stretch my legs into a pasture of bedding, and the untouched cotton is cold on my skin. I try to convince myself it's nice to have this king-size freedom, to sleep at a diagonal and use all five pillows. Whole bed to myself. I get up to brush my teeth, but the toothpaste is gone. I leave my toothbrush and head to the kitchen to make coffee. I pass the dining room table; it's loaded up with drill bits and junk mail and yesterday's protein shake bottle. At the kitchen sink, I see Tyler's toothbrush and the capless tube of toothpaste. Suppressing an urge to slam something, I go instead to grind the coffee beans and with a slow and measured step, I place my heel just so, right on the edge of the toothpaste cap so that the weight of last night's argument sinks down onto the object, lodging it squarely into my foot. Injury to insult.

I look at Tyler asleep on the couch: it's infuriating. The simple domestic existence of this other person has become a hostile act against me somehow. I'm territorial over the couch now, like I was going to sit there but can't. (I wasn't.) I make the coffee. I drink some. I set the pot and a mug in the general couch area, near him. I'm smug, like I did a big, brave act. My brain has the good sense to recommend offering a few words—*Hey, sorry about last night. Can we start over?* But my ego muzzles me, and instead I just look at him. He's wedged face down in the corner of the sofa without a blanket or a real pillow. Still sleeping. Ignoring me! He looks uncomfortable. *Good,* I think. I immediately feel bad for thinking that.

Outside, the morning is full of white fog and quiet. It has a gentleness that makes me feel lonely. With the door at my back, I start to cry. I go to start my day.

Marriage is hard. Working together is also hard. The two are often inseparable challenges that wear us out and test our fortitude. It shocks me—scares me, even—how much easier it would be to quit, to go our individual paths. I've daydreamed about that avenue, rolled around the textures of not answering to anyone, cracking my knuckles whenever I feel like it. It's more familiar to me, being independent, creating a need to survive and then doing it, alone. I know Tyler is wired the same way, and I know we have both imagined leaving in our lowest moments. To be fair, I imagine a lot of things. Sometimes I imagine telling a complete stranger—usually the one who is clipping his fingernails and collecting them in a pile in his lap while seated next to me on an airplane—to get out, to open the door and please jump out of the plane. But I don't do that.

Sometimes I eat half a Popsicle and put it back in the box, and I step out of pants in a way that leaves them sort of still standing, like a ghost is in them, behind the door in the bathroom, which is a very weird, disturbing sight, probably not unlike drill bits on a dining room table. I crunch potato chips in bed. I criticize faucet hardware as my husband is installing it.

I struggle to communicate and fail to realize crucial things about myself, often until it's too late. More times than I care to count, I have blinked awake, unable to see the color of my own eyes, yet refusing to look into the mirror and understand the objective truths my marriage is holding up in front of me.

Ultimately, we make it back to each other. One of us reaches for the other one's hand; we don't want to run. For me, that hand is warm and freckled and attached to a man who willingly gets up at 3 a.m. to take the dog out, because he loves Hudson as much as he loves me; a man who makes the coffee in the morning while I'm still asleep, who builds me shelves and rooms and furniture and whole houses by hand; someone who throws me birthday parties against my will and makes me pizza and reads next to me in bed or at least holds a book up with his eyes closed *as if* he is reading; someone who shows up to do the sometimes demanding work of staying married.

Besides, the fight that leads to waking up in bed alone is never about walking the dog or diverging visions on how to use the garage. The real problem isn't hardware on the table or laundry on the floor, though those things can make you want to burn it all.

The problem, or opportunity, is that marriage will pull the guts of your guts out into the open, and you will have to touch each misunderstood part of yourself and come to realize and accept that you are full of unhealed wounds—broken bones holding baseball bats, lying in wait for the next perceived threat. You have long-held delusions about what marriage even is, and so has the other person. What's more is that your own (flawed) belief system is what undermines you, operating outside your awareness.
You have to slowly learn, and then accept, something so antithetical to your idea of self, and then you have to risk exposing yourself, and then you have to find the capacity to listen to and contemplate the counter-experience, because neither of you—neither of us—is even remotely close to being fully baked.

We've cracked the eggs and tossed them in. We've dragged the flour through the bowl and grated in cold butter, pinching and squeezing it tight; it's nothing, really. Just sticky. Trying to make anything of it only causes it to fall apart worse. It's hard as a rock. It splits. It's finicky, and it exhausts you physically. Somewhere it changes. When you're about to freak out because it'll never be any good, and you're certain you made

an unfixable error, it comes together. And thankfully so, since it's not possible to get the eggs out and tuck them neatly back into their shells like nothing happened.

Pie dough is a lot like that.

(Recipe continues)

PIE DOUGH, SUMMER FRUIT PIE, AND FALL/WINTER APPLE PIE

I learned to make pie dough early in my restaurant life. I was general manager at a good restaurant. Going in, I was not a pie person. I don't think I had even had pie up until that point, unless we count the time my mom forced a bite of spinach quiche on me when I was four; I only tasted that because it looked like dessert and it absolutely was not. Well, I tried the pie we had at this restaurant and I was hypnotized. This pie had summer fruit and a crust so flake-tastic it could have resurrected my dead grandmother (Ro, she had problems with flaky doughs). The crust was what did it for me. Have you ever seen a small child try ice cream for the first time? It's a neurological event.

I don't know how many of these moments you get as an adult, but it was like that—the texture, the flavors, how it all fit together—I wanted to know how. I wanted to be able to make one.

I showed up in the prep kitchen with my notebook at 5:30 a.m. to learn how to make pie dough. The whole experience was remarkably simple—very physical, very specific—but not hard. After that, I made pies every week that summer for practice. Pies heavy with expensive white peaches and strawberries, nectarines and raspberries, blackberries and cherries. The materials to make the pies probably cost me sixty dollars a pie. If you account for inflation, they were worth thousands of dollars. I gave them out for birthdays and Sundays. I fell in love with pies. Romantically. The fruit filling is delightful, but the way the butter cuts into flour is what moves me.

This recipe has never, ever, failed me. I inevitably always think of those early days in my restaurant career and the generosity of the chef when I get out the ingredients. I refer to that same tattered notebook I used over a decade ago. It's my emotional support notebook; it helps the pies know they're safe in my hands. Tyler can't stand to watch me make pie dough because I never weigh anything, only measure, which is in huge violation of baking law. He says I'm doing it wrong. He also says how wonderful my pies are, and always calls them perfect. He's being honest. About all of it.

I will advise you to weigh your ingredients. I just can't practice what I preach.

I would argue that grandmothers all over the world have been eyeballing things like pie dough and doing just fine. Except mine. I never had a grandmother who made pies because, as I mentioned, flaking was a cardinal sin in her house, so my grandfather had to sneak croissants from the bakery in through the garage after having transferred them from the pink box into a plastic bag. Unfortunately, they always left a trail, which was her whole chagrin with things that flake in the first place. He'd get a talking-to every time.

I make this dough by feel now, adjusting water and butter levels as needed, even when scaling it up to make 120 pies during a pandemic (highly ill advised).

Summer is for stone fruit and berry pies because they're in season, an impeccable combination because the pectin in stone fruit balances the liquid created by cooked, macerated berries. In winter, it's apple pie for me. You can use this crust for a great many more kinds of pie, even savory potpies, little flaky biscuit-like bites with no filling, and as the bottom for open-top custard and cream pies, like chocolate or pumpkin, but I don't like to make those. Open-top pies require two bakes. You have to work with parchment paper and some sort of pie weights, like dried beans. Those get all greasy and piping hot, so you burn yourself trying to spread them out evenly because the bottom starts puffing up halfway through the first bake. Then you have to remove insanely hot beans, now unusable for actual food, I think, and wait for the crust to cool before *(Recipe continues)* filling the pies with their filling only to bake them again, and it's already 3 a.m. on the eve of the second Pandemic Thanksgiving but you still have ninety-eight more pies to go, and the oven in the prep kitchen only holds sixteen at a time and all the workspace is fully occupied with hundreds of portions of mashed potatoes and creamed spinach, so you can't spread them out to cool properly and you have to walk them one by one next door to cool, and on the last trip of transferring the last pie, you slip because Converse have no traction, especially not on hot butter, and you drop the entire best-looking pie and nearly quit everything. Let's stick to pies with a top and bottom crust, shall we?

Makes enough for five (9-inch/23 cm) pies, because it's better to have dough on hand than have to make more!

Dough

1 cup (240 ml) filtered water
12 cups (1.5 kg) all-purpose flour, plus extra for rolling
1 tablespoon plus 1 teaspoon salt
3 pounds (1.4 kg) high-quality unsalted frozen butter, such as Plugra
4 large eggs
¼ cup (60 ml) apple cider vinegar
2 ice cubes

Spray bottle
Large bowl
Box grater
Sharp knife
Rolling pin
9-inch (23 cm) glass pie dish
Kitchen paintbrush
Large baking sheet

Summer Fruit Pie Filling

About 12 large peaches, nectarines, apricots, plums, or a mix, pitted and sliced (around 6 cups)

4 cups (560 g) of your favorite berries: blackberries, strawberries (quartered through the stem), boysenberries, salmonberries, whatever you like!
½ cup (100 g) granulated sugar
2 lemons, halved
6 tablespoons (55 g) tapioca pearls (if you're going heavier on berries than stone fruit, increase tapioca pearls by 1 tablespoon; if you're doing just stone fruit, decrease to 4 tablespoons [40 g] total)
2 tablespoons cold unsalted butter, cut into ¼-inch (6 mm) cubes

Fall/Winter Apple Pie Filling

10 to 12 apples, I like a combo of Granny Smith and Honeycrisp, peeled, cored, and sliced into even ¼- to ½-inch-thick (6 to 12 mm) slices (10 cups)
1½ cups (330 g) packed brown sugar
3 tablespoons cornstarch
½ teaspoon freshly grated nutmeg
¼ teaspoon ground cinnamon
½ cup (120 ml) apple juice
Squeeze of fresh lemon juice
8 tablespoons (115 g) unsalted butter

4-quart (3.8 L) saucepan, the wider the better

For assembling the pie

Heavy cream
Turbinado sugar

Make the dough: Put the filtered water in a spray bottle and set aside. Combine the flour and salt in a large bowl. When I say large, I mean triple the size you're probably thinking. Something 24 inches (60 cm) across does nicely. Unwrap your frozen butter and put your box grater in the bowl of dry ingredients, wrap the bottom of your butter in a paper towel so you can hold it, and grate the frozen butter into the bowl (it should look like shredded mozzarella). Pause occasionally to clear out the butter and distribute it over the dry *(Recipe continues)*

ingredients. Once all the butter is grated, start to incorporate the dry mix into the butter. This is called "cutting in" and it's about combining the fat into the dry mix, not to make a paste but rather a shaggy, crumbly situation. It should look like coarse oatmeal. "Shaggy" is the key word. You know how when you make cookies and you cream the butter and sugar into the flour and it gets all smooth? That's NOT the idea. The butter needs to be evenly distributed into the flour mix but retain its shaggy look.

Whisk together the eggs, apple cider vinegar, and ice cubes in a measuring cup. The ice cubes will melt and keep the eggs very cold; if any cubes remain, just toss them out and then pour the egg mix into the shaggy dough mix and roll your hands through the wet mixture to incorporate evenly throughout. It's a small ratio of liquid to dry here, so it might not feel possible. Do it anyway. Mist in the water little by little. As you spray the dough, gently incorporate the water with your hands so that the dough becomes hydrated and sticks in clumps when you grab a fistful of it. The dough should still be flaky but begin to hold together.

Start gathering softball-size portions of dough that weigh 11 ounces (310 g). Since 1 ounce = 1 inch, or 2.5 cm (and we're making a 9-inch [23 cm] pie), 11 ounces gives you 11 inches (28 cm) and that's a nice buffer when rolling. Shape each portion of dough into a ball and then press it into a disc about 1 inch (2.5 cm) thick. Tightly wrap this portion in plastic wrap; if your wrapping job is baggy and loose, berate yourself and do better (or get work as a stage—stagiaire?—aka, a job for zero money at a strict kitchen, and come back in eight months to reattempt this step).

Once the pie dough is portioned and wrapped, refrigerate to rest at least 24 hours and up to 4 days before rolling them out to bake. You can also freeze the portions for 1 month. Thaw them in the fridge the night before you're planning to make pies.

Make the summer fruit pie filling: The day of baking, combine the cut stone fruit and berries in a large bowl. Add the sugar and squeeze the lemon juice into the mix. Toss gently to incorporate, then add the tapioca pearls and gently incorporate. You do not want to beat up and damage the fruit. Let the mixture stand for about 30 minutes and up to 1 hour. The sugar will amplify the flavors of the berries by drawing out their sweet juices and creating a syrup. Scatter the butter cubes into the fruit mix. It's ready to use as filling.

Make the fall/winter apple pie filling: There's a device for peeling and slicing apples, and it's sort of like a cavatelli maker, which is to say it's hand-cranking, very dangerous, impossible to clean, and generally breaks after one to three uses. I like them but usually can't find the one I have or don't have one anymore because it broke. Setting up the device feels like more work up front, but you get nice, evenly peeled and sliced apples and have less waste (of apples, not time).

If your husband makes fun of you for using such a device, or you don't have one, just peel them the old-fashioned way, then slice them with a knife. Even thickness on your slices is crucial. Cooking the apples ahead of time prevents them from becoming mushy in the pie-baking phase. You get al dente apples, not applesauce, and this step is really the key to the whole thing, and the most impressive.

Combine the brown sugar, cornstarch, nutmeg, and cinnamon in a bowl and set aside.

Get a 4-quart (3.8 L) saucepan over medium-high heat. Add the sliced apples, apple juice, and lemon juice and stir occasionally for 5 to 8 minutes. Add the butter and stir until it's melted. Once melted, add the brown sugar mixture and stir. *(Recipe continues)*

The sauce will begin to thicken. Stir constantly, and turn the heat a bit higher to get it bubbling to thicken and reduce. You're essentially making a caramel, but with a cornstarch accelerator. Carefully taste and make sure it's sweetly balanced but not cloying and not overly starchy. The apples should be cooked but not mushy; remove from the heat just before you think they're done. Spread the apples on a sheet pan to cool and, once warm or room temperature, transfer to a bowl and cover with plastic wrap or put in an airtight container and store in the fridge for a few hours and up to 4 days ahead.

Assembling and baking the pie: Take dough portions (two per pie) out of the fridge: in summer they need to sit at room temperature for about 25 minutes before rolling; in winter, you can take them out 45 minutes before rolling. They should be soft enough to work with but still firm and cold. Dough that's too warm won't roll out.

Preheat the oven to 425°F (215°C).

Prepare a clean, open workspace on a smooth surface. Sprinkle flour over the work area and rolling pin. Flour your hands. Unwrap the portions of dough and work them in your hands to shape each one into a larger, flatter circle. Once the dough is about half as thick and hopefully still round, sprinkle with flour and begin to roll. Roll from the center out, and turn the dough a tick to the right each time you roll out. (If the pie dough is the face of a clock, each turn should be about three seconds, so not a lot.) This keeps the dough from sticking and lets you know when to add flour to keep preventing it from doing so. Rolling out from the center will keep you forming a circle, so roll, turn, roll, turn. Once the dough is nearly the right size for the pie pan, I sometimes roll the dough from the center out in various directions without rotating it. Once the dough is about 10 inches (25 cm) across and ⅛ inch

(3 mm) thick, stop rolling. Too thin and it will rip, too thick and it won't bake properly.

To assemble: Once both portions are rolled out and look absolutely identical and perfectly round (kidding, this won't happen but it's okay!), it's time to build the pie. Place one portion in the center of the pie dish. If one piece of dough has a tear or feels less perfect, use that one for the bottom of the pie. You can patch a tear in the bottom with a scrap of dough, no problem!

Gently press the rolled dough into the walls of the pie dish and let the edges drape over. If it's hot out, put the other portion of dough on wax (or butcher or parchment) paper and store in the fridge.

Scoop the fruit filling into the bottom of the pie using a large slotted spoon or your hands. Stack a large mound of fruit in the center, so as to make a mountain of fruit twice the height of the pie dish with sides that are flush with the edge of the dish.

Use your finger and dab a small amount of cream on the top edge of the dough, going around the pie dish, where the top crust will marry the bottom one and make a seal. Drape the top crust over the filling and let it connect with the bottom crust and hang over the edges of the pie pan.

It's important that the edges are sealed. If there is a lot of overhang, trim the excess with the sharp knife, going around the dish and leaving enough that the edges are equal and extend slightly over the dish, but just barely. Now a few options: Pressing the edges with the tines of a fork or the end of a butter knife is easy and makes a nice textured pattern. You can also scallop the edges by pressing your index finger into your opposite hand's index and thumb fingers, which will create a gentle wave—a little harder but still not too hard (there are videos on the internet). You *(Recipe continues)*

can pinch the layers together to seal and then form a flat crust. Just make sure it's sealed.

Brush the excess flour off the top crust with the kitchen paintbrush.. Dip your brush in the heavy cream and paint the pie with it. I specifically do not like egg wash—I find it stains your hard work with the unpleasant smell of eggs. Sprinkle the raw sugar over the top evenly for a nice sweet crunch.

Vent your pie with the very tiny, very sharp knife. Find the center of the top of the pie and imagine a quarter on that center spot. Begin your cut at the edge of the quarter, making a straight line and stop 3 inches (7.5 cm) from the edge of the pie pan. Be careful, don't cut through to the bottom of the pie. Repeat this so you have four lines that are quartering the top of the pie equally. Make one smaller cut in between each of the longer four lines, so you have eight total vents radiating from the center—four long, four short. This divides the pie into eight theoretical slices, which is also nice. Feel free to express yourself as long as you do not cut the bottom crust or make big holes. Venting simply allows air to escape during the baking process, so it doesn't explode. It gets hot inside of a pie!

To bake: Carefully place the assembled pie on a large sheet pan. This is helpful for when some of the juicy fruit filling inevitably spews out of the vents (or an edge that wasn't fully pinched!) or the butter drips. Hot butter and sugar hit the bottom of the oven and create smoke, lots of it. That's how you can make your pie taste like BBQ. I learned this the hard way when I baked several pies at home for the restaurant and then served up a weird amalgamation that was probably a flavor of gum in the Willy Wonka factory; I think it's called Strawberry-Peach Smoky Texas Tri-Tip. It was not tasty. The sheet pan is your ally.

Bake the pie for about 20 minutes, then drop the temperature to 375°F (190°C). Let it go for another 40 minutes—DON'T OPEN THE OVEN! The pie is done when the crust is evenly cooked and golden but not burned. You may need to keep it in the oven for up to 20 minutes longer. Check it periodically for a golden-brown crust. Cool for at least 5 hours before serving.

GATEAU BASQUE

If you're going to tell a story, I bet you'd start at the beginning. In this case, I can't. I just don't remember the first basque. I do know for certain that the first cake was baked on June 6, and Tyler's made this cake for my birthday every year since—but *since when*, as I said, remains uncertain. Truthfully, I don't even remember the first meal he ever made me, just many nights around a fire where he'd be roasting fish or pork and charring corn in denim cutoffs in the middle of another Los Angeles heat wave. Tyler has been cooking for me since way before we were a couple, including this basque.

He would cream butter and sugar by hand in lieu of a mixer. Or central air. In June. He amassed dozens of baking hours (plus five years, depending on which story he's telling) at an unhurried pace foreign to an impatient man like himself. Even if we never got together, he later told me, it was lovely just to be in love no matter the outcome.

As far as history goes, our story begins with that first cake I can't properly file into linear time. I imagine nesting rings of pastry cream unfurling from that point, each subsequent basque its own ring, marking the passage of time and our slow evolution into an eventual couple. Like a tree, only cake.

These days, when we gather on June 6, people have by now heard the folklore of Tyler's basque. When it parades out adorned with lit candles, first-timers look skeptical. I can tell they're judging its plain appearance. It's true, the cake looks simple, austere even. They say things preemptively, like "Oh, I'm not really a cake person" and "I don't love sweets," making sure they're not obligated to finish a slice or even try it.

But believe me, they always do.

When the cake is cut, the crust cracks open and shows off a fine crumb, not too course or too tightly packed, merged with invisible coiled layers of pastry cream. To separate crumb from cream would be like trying to find the exact location where sand becomes sea—impossible. The basque is as emblematic of summer as the beach itself. And what is summer for, if not the prospect of falling in love?

Second slices are generally not permitted. Tradition mandates enough cake must remain to have a slice for breakfast with my coffee the next couple mornings. I like to do this while I reflect on the general splendidness of life. Over the next day or two, I go to the fridge, I unwrap the foil, I slice off a corner with a butter knife, and I sit down at the table with my coffee and cake. I savor the evolution—it goes from fridge-cold to soft, yielding as it warms. Once, there was no cake left and I had to have a scone on June 7 and it wasn't the same. Tyler now makes backup cakes to ensure the law of leftovers is upheld. It's a miracle of science what can fit in a 9-inch (23 cm) diameter. Even a single slice has a great deal more heft than its square footage implies. I like to think it's a testament to all that's in there, besides the butter and eggs.

Now we are married, and each year on Gateau Basque Day I eat this cake and think of our love story. Good luck with the recipe. You'll need it, along with some fortitude and patience, and unbridled romance. I wish you all of the above.

GATEAU BASQUE (ASHLEY'S BIRTHDAY CAKE)

It's strange that people have been making Ashley's birthday cake for *(Recipe continues)*

hundreds of years before she was born. That tells you what you should know about her, I guess.

This is the best cake I've ever had, and it's a huge mess to make. For some reason, I always refused to use a mixer, some sort of bizarre measure to prove my love through suffering. You should definitely use one (I do, now—we're married). There's never quite enough batter and way too much pastry cream. I make it only once a year to commemorate Ashley's birthday. I turn off the phone and draw the shades. I can't be bothered while it's under way. This cake is a half-day affair, requiring a small amount of skill, some organization, patience—all of which I have very little of—and faith that you'll attain great success and get to the other side.

A Moment on Custards

Of all the custard preparations, pastry cream is the most forgiving. Once you understand the why of pastry cream, or any custard, then you're working *with* the ingredients and everyone wins. Here's a primer:

Custard is just a dairy base thickened with eggs. Old-school ice cream, crème brûlée, lemon curd, flan—yep, all custards. Heating egg yolks until they provide the thickening power without making scrambled eggs is the crux of the operation. Pastry cream works the same, but we get training wheels (cornstarch). Cornstarch allows a little more flexibility in temperature and technique, and it helps make a stiffer custard.

A digital thermometer sure helps, but it's not crucial. The most important step is bringing the eggs up to temperature slowly. This is called tempering. After that, like anything in life, you can force your mistakes through a fine-mesh strainer.

We'll make the pastry cream first since it needs to cool before we assemble the cake. You can also make this a day or two ahead.

Serves 6 to 8

Pastry Cream
....

4 cups (960 ml) heavy cream
½ cup (100 g) granulated sugar
9 large egg yolks
⅓ cup (50 g) cornstarch
¼ cup (½ stick/55 g) unsalted butter, cubed
3 tablespoons vanilla paste
1 teaspoon kosher salt

Gateau
....

1 pound (4 sticks/455 g) unsalted butter, at room temperature, plus more for greasing
1 pound (455 g) granulated sugar
2 teaspoons vanilla paste
3 large eggs, at room temperature
Scant 4 cups (480 g) cake or all-purpose flour
2 teaspoons baking powder
1 tablespoon kosher salt

Tools
....

Heavy-bottomed, 4-quart (3.8 L) or larger saucepan
3 medium bowls
Whisk
Rubber spatula (optional)
Ladle or measuring cup
Fine-mesh strainer
Digital or candy thermometer (optional)
Stand mixer (or some core strength and patience, plus a wooden spoon and a large bowl, and Tiger Balm)
Pastry bag (optional; a zip-tight one with the corner cut off gets the job done but not nearly as well)
8- or 9-inch (20 or 23 cm) springform pan
Parchment paper (optional)

Make the pastry cream: Put the cream and granulated sugar in the saucepan on medium heat. Heating cream with *(Recipe continues)* sugar helps prevent the cream from scalding. While it's heating, put the egg yolks in a medium bowl and whisk until light and foamy, about 1 minute. Whisk in the cornstarch. It should become thick and difficult to whisk. That's good.

Once the milk has reached "ouch, that's hot" on your finger, or about 140°F (60°C), we'll begin the tempering process. Use a ladle to scoop out about ½ cup (120 ml) of the hot milk and pour it into the egg yolk–cornstarch mixture. Whisk vigorously while you do. Add another ½ cup (120 ml) and keep whisking. And once more.

At this point, you have a nice warm mixture in the bowl. Pour the whole mix back into the saucepan and stir constantly with a whisk or rubber spatula. The pastry cream will cook at the bottom first, so you have to stir it tirelessly and watch out for solid bits. It will begin to set up pretty quickly, which is good. We're looking for the consistency of pudding plus a little bit. When you think it's done, cook it for 15 more seconds.

As soon as you take it off the heat, pour it through the fine-mesh strainer into a clean medium bowl. You can use the whisk or spatula to make sure you get it all through there. Sorry about the mess.

Add the butter, vanilla paste, and salt to the hot, strained pastry cream and stir until it's all incorporated. At this point, I find it's very important to taste a spoonful approximately every 30 seconds until you don't feel very good.

Some say to put plastic wrap on the surface, to prevent a skin from forming while it cools. You can, but I don't. I prefer to put the pastry cream in the fridge to cool completely (keep it in the bowl) and stir it every few minutes until it's cool to avoid that, maybe 30 minutes. You can let it cool in the freezer, too, just don't

let it freeze. Now's a good time to wash your dishes; next comes the easy part.

Make the gateau: If you have a stand mixer, you should use it; if you don't, I salute you. You'll want to use the paddle attachment.

Add the butter, granulated sugar, and vanilla paste. Mix on low, then increase the speed to medium as it comes together, and then go up to medium high for about 2 minutes. We want smooth creamed butter and sugar. Creaming is integral to baking! It's not merely combining things, but aerating the two ingredients into a single, fluffy component; it's the reason a chocolate chip cookie can attain a gentle, chewy center and a crisp, crunchy edge simultaneously—those crevices between the crumbs, that subtle, airy void of negative space is born of the art that is properly creamed butter and sugar.

Reduce the mixer to low and add the eggs, one at a time, until each is incorporated. Mix the flour, baking powder, and salt in a separate, clean medium bowl and add one-third at a time until just barely mixed. Overmixing flour in a cake or cookies is a common mistake that results in chewy, tough baked goods. You didn't come this far to overmix!

It's also important to taste this cake batter until you're not sure there's enough to even bake the cake and you start feeling sick, in a good way. I've housed so much of this batter over the years and nothing bad has happened, but here's your OREA (obligatory raw egg advisory): Don't follow my lead if you're the cautious type.

And now, assembly. Full disclosure: This is a frustrating process but trust the cake! She will provide.

We're essentially constructing a bowl out of the cake batter, then filling that with the pastry cream, and then making a *(Recipe continues)*

156

cake batter lid. I've done this part a couple ways. You can do it with a pastry bag, but the best method is to use your hands.

Preheat the oven to 375°F (190°C) and butter the springform pan. If you can figure out how to cut a parchment into a circle that fits on the bottom of your pan, congratulations! It's helpful but not absolutely necessary. It's important to make sure the sides and bottom of the pan are properly greased with butter, as well as the parchment itself (if using).

With wet hands, scoop some batter from the bowl into the springform. Press it flat and up the sides of the pan, creating a reservoir that comes two-thirds of the way up the side of the pan. It'll take a few handfuls, and you'll use about half the dough.

Fill the center with the cooled pastry cream. It should be smooth and kind of pourable, like the texture of Greek yogurt. It's very forgiving, so believe in whatever you made! It should come two-thirds up the side of the pan. You have some headroom, and now you're going to finish the cake with more batter. This part is basically impossible. I finally figured out that with the wet-hands method, you can make four or five rafts out of batter and lay them side by side across the top. I've never successfully covered every square millimeter of the pastry cream so don't worry. Just do your best. The cake will rise when it bakes and miraculously fill in the spaces.

Lift with your legs and put the springform pan on a sheet pan and into the oven. It's going to drip so it's crucial to have the sheet pan under the cake. Bake it until it develops a beautiful dark crust, has an incredible aroma, and sets up so there's no jiggle in the middle. At least an hour. Sometimes longer. Ideally, you'll rest it for several hours before cutting into it, but you're an adult and we trust you.

If there's extra batter, you can grease some muffin tins and make mini individual cakes—and since they're the shape of a muffin, they are now a viable breakfast. Bake at the same temperature, and start checking for doneness at around the 20-minute mark.

This cake is probably good for a few days in the refrigerator at least, but we've never made it last for more than two.

PAUL'S CHOCOLATE CAKE

Paul came in one day and said he felt like a chocolate cake. Then I started craving a chocolate cake. Then one appeared on the menu. Paul is sneaky like that. I can't remember the details. All we know is that once it arrived, a legend was born. You make the cake, the mousse, and the ganache separately, and assemble the parts to order, or in this case, to serve. Like how moms make nachos in the toaster oven for you on some foil as an afterschool snack or even dinner. I know Tyler's mom made them so that each single chip got its own treatment, topped individually with a lot of care and shredded cheese, and this cake is of similar methodology. Trying to make one big cake to cut into slices isn't worth it; it can't be done, it's flat-out wrong. Repeating: Don't try to shortcut this recipe by making one large cake. It'll be the long way around to a huge mess and no cake to eat (or soothe the feelings of failure).

Paul said his inspiration was a chocolate cake that was not the deli-case frosted cake of nostalgia, but one that was equally satisfying. It couldn't be overly cerebral with superfluousness like lavender and black pepper and cayenne. What he came up with is a no-frills cake, texturally incredible, not too sweet, one that over delivers every time. Like Paul himself. I always think I'll have just one bite but then I can't stop. Tyler doesn't have that problem. Meaning he doesn't think he'll stop after one bite because he can eat three whole cakes. Sometimes we want this cake so badly that we'll go ask Paul (who's simultaneously working on the line and expediting because a cook called out again) to make us a one-bite cake. He'll pretend he's not going to, but then he'll cut five mini squares of cake and surgically layer mousse in between each one and make us a very tall tiny cake tower, because he's a saint and a father and a softie and a dry-witted British man. This cake reminds me of those old-fashioned ice cream sandwiches, the ones that stick to your fingers. I guess you could top it with nuts or something crunchy, but we don't do that. It's already perfect. Good job, Paul.

One (9 x 13-inch / 23 x 33 cm) cake; makes 6 to 8 large portions

Cake

220 grams all-purpose flour
60 grams cocoa powder
350 grams granulated sugar
2 teaspoons baking soda
1 teaspoon baking powder
1 teaspoon kosher salt
2 teaspoons espresso powder
100 grams (120 ml) extra-virgin olive oil
2 large eggs
180 grams sour cream
125 grams (120 ml) buttermilk
2 teaspoons vanilla extract
100 grams (120 ml) fresh brewed coffee
Flaky sea salt

Caramel Mousse

225 grams Valrhona Dulcey (35% cacao) beurre de cacao pistoles; Valrhona is the best quality and just superior for melting
240 grams (240 ml) hot heavy cream (135°F/55°C)
240 grams (240 ml) cold heavy cream
2 tablespoons confectioners' sugar

Ganache

285 grams semisweet good-quality melting chocolate (we use 55% cacao); don't use chocolate chips—they are *(Recipe continues)*

designed to hold their shape and won't melt as well

480 grams (480 ml) hot heavy cream (135°F/55°C)

Make the cake: Preheat the oven to 350°F (175°C) and butter a 9 x 13-inch (23 x 33 cm) baking dish. Combine the dry ingredients in a large bowl and set aside. In another bowl, combine the wet ingredients except the fresh-brewed coffee, then mix the coffee in last. Add the wet ingredients into the dry and mix slowly to combine.

Pour the cake batter into the baking dish; it should be two-thirds full. Bake for 15 minutes, then check it with your cake tester; when it comes out clean or almost clean, the cake's done! It's better to slightly under- than over-bake, as it will cool to doneness and this is one cake you want to be nice and spongy, not dry.

Make the caramel mousse: Put the Dulcey pistoles in a glass heat-resistant bowl and pour the hot cream over them. Let sit for 5 minutes, then whisk until smooth. Allow to cool.

Put the chilled heavy cream in a mixing bowl and add the confectioners' sugar. Whisk until stiff peaks form, meaning you can turn the bowl upside down and it won't fall out. A cold bowl, a cold whisk, and cold cream will help speed the process. You can also use a mixer on medium high. Fold 350 grams of the whipped cream into the melted, cooled Dulcey, using a spatula to incorporate. Refrigerate. You want the mousse to be cold and scoopable. The mousse can be made a few days ahead and stored in an airtight container in the fridge. Take it out just when you're ready to assemble the cakes.

Make the ganache: Put the chocolate in a nice big bowl and pour the hot cream over it. Let sit for 5 minutes, then whisk until smooth. This is your finishing sauce, so once you assemble the cakes, you'll pour this over the top.

Assemble the cake: Once this trifecta of elements is prepared and the cake has cooled, it's time to assemble. Use a knife to divide the cake in the pan into nine 3-inch (7.5 cm) squares. Now cut each square in half horizontally, the way you'd approach a bagel, so you have eighteen squares that are about 1 inch (2.5 cm) high and 3 inches (7.5 cm) per side. These are your layers, and you need three layers per portion, so that's six portions (you should read the text message exchange between Paul and me on the math for this one to scale the recipe—it's a dialogue with about fifteen rounds of equations back and forth, trying to convert this recipe for a non-restaurant prep portion, culminating in the final, mature exchange):

> **Paul:** "Trust me it's enough; 3 inches by 3 inches is HUGE."
>
> **Me:** "That's what you want me to think."

One "slice" can be split between two or more people, though some (Tyler) can take down a whole portion; he's not alone. We have plenty of regulars who come in on a date and order two cakes. I myself have done it. One night, I was expediting and hadn't eaten all day. At 10 p.m. all I could think about was this cake. I had been seeing and smelling orders of it get plated all night long. When dinner service was finally over, I ate a whole portion (3 x 3 x 4 inches/ 7.5 x 7.5 x 10 cm) with two glasses of wine. Okay, three glasses. A very I'm-an-adult-and-*can*-actually-do-whatever-I-want moment! I slept absolutely horribly and couldn't tell if my hangover was from sugar or wine (yes); it was totally worth it.

Okay, it's time to start building the cakes! Place one square of cake in the center of the plate. Using an ice cream scoop or large spoon, drop a roughly 2-ounce (60 ml) portion of mousse into the center of the base layer. Place the second layer of cake on top, gently pressing to secure while keeping the height. Drop a second scoop of mousse on the second layer, and top it with another square of cake, the third and final layer.

Stir the ganache, which should be pourable and smooth, and pour slowly over the top. Don't drown the cake! Just cover the top square sufficiently and let it drip over the cliff of cake. If your ganache is too hot, it won't stick to the cake properly, and if it's too cold it won't pour evenly. It should be room temp. Finish with some nice flaky salt. If you're serving more than one portion, assemble the layers of all portions, and then ganache them all at the end, just before you serve dessert.

WHITE CHOCOLATE RASPBERRY CHEESECAKE

In the college days, my mom would pull up into the giant university parking lot while I stood on the dorm steps. She'd stop mid-lane and roll down the passenger window of her Camry to wave to me while a bouquet of balloons assaulted her from the back seat. Her giant smile was eclipsed in size by her enormous sunglasses. I'd spot a wrapped gift on the seat next to her, something I'd have order-fired myself, and also the big get: The Greatest Cheesecake of All Time (meaning of life in general, because All Time the restaurant was not yet born). It sat beside her for the drive up from San Diego. She'd personally escorted it (and buckled it in) on the passenger seat for its two-hour journey from the aptly named Incredible Cheesecake Company. God, I miss her.

If it's still there, the bakery sits in an always-gray neighborhood on a small side street overlooking a San Diego freeway, and it pumps out a disproportionately vast number of cheesecake flavors for its tiny storefront. So many flavors. I'll never know how lemon or caramel chip taste, because my mom and I never strayed from white chocolate raspberry. In solidarity, I never will.

Our cake had twirls of gorgeous white and dark chocolate shavings that never made it home to be eaten as part of the complete cake experience. On the drive, I would pluck each delicate curl, one by one, while my mom scolded me to restrain myself so we could get home, do the candles, have the cake as a whole. I couldn't. This habit harkens back to my high school days, when I'd hear my mom yell my name in exasperation from the kitchen because she'd found a half granola bar upside down in its wrapper back in its box, when she was going for the whole (glutenous!) granola bar. Much to Tyler's dismay, old habits die hard: I admit I'll open a can of something sparkling, take a sip,

and restore it to its position in the fridge under the delusion that it will be both finished (never) and carbonated (impossible) later. I like to think of myself as an Elaine, but everyone has a few Kramer tendencies if you look objectively in the mirror, and I'm aware of my own, which stop short, just barely, of a bowl of IOUs.

Maybe you think, how lazy and unmotherly to *buy* a cake instead of making one from scratch (and also to serve me a slice for breakfast before school, which happened every year until I left for college). Incorrect. I've spent the better part of my adult life craving this cake and the memory of it is so linked to my mom and her big drugstore sunglasses and birthday voicemails and distinct, slanted handwriting in the cards that came reliably every year, that it has always felt like this cake is just ours, that no one else ever bought that flavor, and that she did make it, just for us.

Tyler tasted this cake when my mom was still alive. She'd bring it up and it would sit on the table next to Gateau Basque, a gentle, sweet stand-off, weighted with butter and love, I guess. He agreed this cheesecake was legit.

Besides all of his other superpowers, Tyler can extract a random, entirely private passing thought I'm having out of my head and put it onto a plate. If I'm craving a quesadilla, I'll walk into the kitchen where he'll be standing over a generously filled tortilla bubbling in a hot pan; if I'm missing Rome, he'll suggest spaghetti for dinner, or make cacio e pepe out of the blue without so much as a word spoken between us.

This one winter, I was missing my mom the excruciatingly normal amount, plus some extra. It was during the pandemic. We were exhausted, very frayed. It *(Recipe continues)*

was Christmas Eve. We were about out the door after work, thanking our staff and also our lucky stars for a restaurant half day (nine hours), when Tyler said he had something to give me. In the parking lot, he presented me with his homemade white chocolate raspberry cheesecake. I get choked up typing this sentence because this gesture and, subsequently, the cake, was so filled with what I was missing that it can't really be captured in words.

He winged it (he always does) and excused the aesthetics and first-time-around quality of the most perfect cake I could imagine.

We ate it that night after a dinner of homemade egg rolls, lo mein, and pickles while watching *Fantastic Mr. Fox*. I'm certain that this is also where traditions begin, which is to say at the intersection of what's essential, what you're missing, and what you're most craving.

WHITE CHOCOLATE RASPBERRY CHEESECAKE

I was reluctant to write this recipe since I had made it only once and we don't make anything close to this thing at the restaurant. Apparently, it was delicious. I remembered it pretty fondly but figured I made a cheesecake, I didn't split the atom. Fireworks emoji, end of story. But Ashley has a way of charming you into doing what she wants. Plus, it wasn't really the end of the story.

It's a funny thing when you lose someone. There are little reminders that creep in and break your heart again when you aren't expecting it. Ashley's mom, Cyndy, would bring this particular cheesecake from a place in San Diego. I knew this cake was one of those things that Ashley had a certain nostalgia about—probably less so about eating cake than the fact that her mom wouldn't be ferrying it to LA annually anymore, but when in doubt I generally get to

work in the kitchen. I didn't quite understand the place this cake holds in both of our hearts as a very sweet reminder of Ashley's mom until I started tearing up while writing this.

A few years ago, on one of the holidays (I sort them according to which annual 9-pound [4 kg] pastry I'm making specifically for Ashley) during that pandemic that was going around, we weren't hosting and no one was showing up at our door with a white chocolate raspberry cheesecake, and it was a really sad time all around. It was the so-called holidays, hard enough as is, but tradition is another one of those peculiarities because when you've lost someone, your mom especially, the traditions linked specifically to her get yanked away, too, however small they are— and it hurts (ask me how I know). I think it's important to try to take a tradition that could be in jeopardy of slipping away and protect it but also make it our own. I feel responsible for making sure we uphold some of the little rituals unique to our moms, for comfort and also just to keep remembering them. For me that's the cobbler; for Ashley, a Chinese food Christmas and a cheesecake seemed appropriate. I figured I could cobble something together based on the "few" that I'd eaten, plus my eight weeks of pastry instruction at Pennsylvania Culinary Institute circa 2002.

Years later (the other day) I made it again. I went from memory and guesswork; I didn't write down a recipe the first time around. I mean, it's a couple pounds of cream cheese and sugar and Oreo crust—this thing is going to be pretty good even if you eat all of the ingredients raw—but this cake was spectacular. I tweaked some things and finally got around to writing it down, and it's so good that I think you should make this every once in a while, too. You'll want to make it the day before you plan to eat it. It's not very hard. A little messy but totally worth it.

Crust

75 grams unsalted butter, plus more for
   greasing the pan
40 chocolate sandwich cookies

White Chocolate Ganache

100 grams good white chocolate (we use
   Valrhona)
75 grams (75 ml) heavy cream

Raspberry Sauce

200 grams raspberries (frozen is fine)
50 grams confectioners' sugar

Cake

910 grams cream cheese
200 grams granulated sugar
1 vanilla bean or 1 tablespoon high-quality
   vanilla paste or extract
5 large eggs
140 grams (140 ml) heavy cream
Good-quality white and dark chocolate
   bars (optional)

Tools

9-inch (23 cm) springform pan with 3- or
   4-inch (7.5 or 10 cm) sides
Food processor or blender
Medium bowl
1 small saucepan that you'll wash and reuse
   a few times
Microwave-safe bowl
Rubber spatula
Stand mixer
Foil
Baking sheet
Small knife
Cooling rack

Make the crust: Preheat the oven to 350°F
(175°C) and butter the springform pan.

Blend the cookies in a food processor or
blender, filling and all, until crumbly like
coarse sand; transfer to a medium bowl. Melt
the butter in a small saucepan over medium
heat, then mix it into the cookies. Press the
cookie mixture into the bottom and about
halfway up the sides of the springform pan in
an even-ish layer.

Bake for 10 minutes and set aside to cool.
Reduce the oven heat to 300°F (150°C).

Make the white chocolate ganache: Put the
white chocolate and cream in a microwave-
safe bowl, and microwave at 50% power in
30-second intervals until it stirs together
smoothly. No microwave? No problem! Put
the white chocolate in a medium bowl. Heat
the cream in a small saucepan until it just
starts to bubble. Pour the hot cream over the
white chocolate and stir together with a rubber
spatula until it's smooth.

Make the raspberry sauce: Cook the
raspberries in a small saucepan over medium
heat until they start to break down, a few
minutes. Add the confectioners' sugar and cook
for another 6 to 7 minutes, stirring frequently.
We're looking for a loosely held together yet
pourable raspberry mixture.

Make the cake: Place the cream cheese,
sugar, and vanilla in the bowl of a stand
mixer with the paddle attachment. Mix
on medium speed for 5 to 7 minutes,
occasionally scraping down the sides and the
bottom with a spatula. The mixture should
be light, fluffy, and room temperature.

Add the eggs, one at a time. Incorporate each
one on medium speed before adding the next,
about 45 seconds per egg. Add the heavy cream
and mix on low for another minute to combine.

Wrap the lower half of your springform in foil.
Do this twice to eliminate the need for a water
bath. People swear that you   *(Recipe continues)*

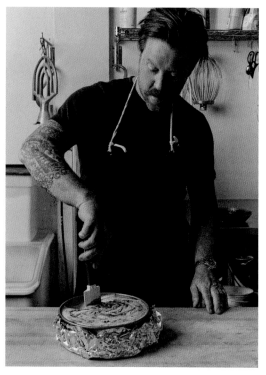

must cook a cheesecake in a water bath, but I haven't found this to be true. I have found water baths to be wet and really messy and sort of dangerous. I think the foil helps insulate the cake from direct heat and I haven't had any problems with my proprietary foil method.

Put the springform pan on a baking sheet, since it's likely to drip. Pour in the batter, stopping about ½ inch (12 mm) from the top or sooner if you run out of batter. Lower is okay; any higher probably not so much.

Pour on the ganache and then the raspberry sauce. Using a small knife or spatula, swirl the raspberries and chocolate into the batter, being careful to not disturb the crust. Don't go nuts, it should take about 20 seconds and feel artistic.

Carefully place the baking sheet on the middle rack of the oven. Bake for 1 hour 20 minutes. It won't be done yet, but it's a good amount of time to clean up half the mess you made and admire your work. Turn the sheet pan 180 degrees at this point. All ovens vary, so I would start checking with a cake tester in another 20 minutes. Be prepared to bake this cake for 20 minutes more, checking with a cake tester every 5 minutes. The cake is done when the cake tester comes out clean; be prepared to go 2 to 2½ hours.

Carefully transfer to a cooling rack and allow it to cool for at least 3 hours before putting in the refrigerator. The cake should spend at least 8 hours in the fridge before serving. When you're ready to serve, gently release the sides of the springform.

If you're feeling fancy or maybe trying to impress your parole officer, or your wife who has the memory of an elephant and houses pastries like one, too, use a vegetable peeler and pull some chocolate curls off of a high-quality chocolate bar for garnish. Both white and dark if you can, that's what I'm told is best.

I've served this cake without a garnish, to show off that it didn't crack but also because it's already maximum decadence.

THE CHOCOLATE CHIP COOKIES OF ALL TIME

I've never caught anyone diving in our dumpster for food. Kind of a non sequitur, but there was an era when an ambitious scavenger, human or otherwise, could have fattened themselves up for several winters on our perfected dumpster cookies. These were the ones that came out only 97 percent good enough. Interestingly, I don't think Ashley, Paul, or I have ever taken anything, personally or professionally, as seriously as these cookies. As such, we've baked thousands for the trash can. At some point, I became a hippie. It happened so gradually that the day someone pointed it out to me I couldn't defend myself. I also grew up poor. The intersection of those things means a strong aversion to wasting food and money. It's a conundrum of the highest order for someone with my compulsions. I have a true emotional response to being wasteful. But I have an even larger pit in my stomach when something leaves the kitchen that could have been better (not that it's ever happened). We found ourselves in need of seemingly endless research and development.

The chocolate chip cookie is also an icon. We had this image of the ideal cookie, and we couldn't compromise. But the thing is, ovens are fickle. Prep cooks sometimes take perceived shortcuts (end destination: baking more cookies), add too much chocolate, overmix the dough, or do a little improv on the recipe. We tried many different kinds of chocolate. Our purveyors to this day might randomly sub our chosen chocolate without letting us know, sometimes for a lesser chocolate. Baking also demands odd subtlety, like the right dough temperature and slamming sheet pans at the exact right moment. In the process of all that process, we learned a lot. We got our asses kicked by cookies, but we got up again. They were never going to keep us down. We honed and honed and the cookies are better than ever. I hope you'll agree that this here is one fine chocolate chip cookie.

Makes 24 to 30 cookies

800 grams all-purpose flour
1 tablespoon kosher salt
¾ tablespoon baking soda
450 grams (1 pound) unsalted butter, at room temperature
350 grams granulated sugar
350 grams brown sugar
4 large eggs, at room temperature
200 grams delicious chocolate chips—we use Valrhona 66% cacao discs; you can use old-school chips, chop up some of your favorite chocolate, whatever you like!
Flaky sea salt

In a large bowl, mix together the flour, salt, and baking soda and set aside.

In a stand mixer with the paddle attachment, or in a large mixing bowl with a hand mixer or by hand, if that's your only option, cream the butter and sugars together. That is to say, mix them for around 3 minutes on medium-high speed until light and fluffy. Add the eggs, one at a time. Mix each egg on medium for about 45 seconds per egg.

On low speed, add the flour mixture, one-third at a time, until each addition is just barely incorporated. Add the chocolate and mix for about 30 seconds. Overmixing cookie dough is a huge sin and the church of pastry requires making an offering to the garbage when you do, so take this step as scripture.

Ashley prefers her cookies Pittsburgh rare, which is to say raw, and I'm inclined to agree. If you have the patience to *(Recipe continues)* see this through, portion the cookie dough that you haven't yet eaten (hopefully half is left at least?) into 75-gram balls. Once portioned, refrigerate them, covered with plastic wrap or in an airtight container, for 3 hours before baking; they can store in the fridge up to 5 days. The dough can also be portioned and then frozen for up to 2 months, stored in a sealed container or plastic bags. Cookies need to be evenly spaced when baking; however, if you're storing them, they can sit close. Whatever the case, they absolutely must bake from round and cold (frozen works): The cookies will bake more evenly and will retain layers of texture, and there are about a thousand other scientific reasons.

Preheat the oven to 325°F (160°C).

Once ready to bake, evenly space the cookies on a baking sheet and do not flatten them. Bake for 10 minutes. Remove the baking sheet and slam it in a single, confident whack on the counter. A direct, solid, straight-down thud to drop the center of the cookie, creating the proprietary crackly top. Yes, it's dangerous.

Rotate the baking sheet and return it to the oven for another 5 to 15 minutes; that's the range—they bake in 12 minutes at the restaurant, but the same recipe takes 25 minutes at our home, and we have a nice oven (sorry, not bragging); you need to monitor them. When they look golden at the edges but appear underdone in the center, take the pan out of the oven and give them another whack on the counter. Rest them on the baking sheet for 5 minutes, then transfer to a cooling rack. Sprinkle some flaky salt over the top and do some jumping jacks or something since you're about to eat way too many.

BROWN BUTTER OATMEAL COOKIES

These cookies happened while I was in the midst of trying to hack the childhood oatmeal cookie recipe that Ashley grew up with from some famed sandwich shop in San Diego. Those cookies are damn good, but they remain a mystery because we struck gold along the way with these.

It's commonly known at work that I have a sweet tooth. It's actually a fang. I try to keep it under control but then inevitably, at the end of lunch service, some young buck who looks like he benches 225 and clearly hasn't for one second in his life considered the consequences of blood sugar piles up all of the unsold cookies and muffins and scones and sets them on the bar like some kind of diabetic double dare. We all walk by and take "just a bite." Over and over. I will go back to break another piece off of an oatmeal cookie on many returns to this trough, convincing myself each bite it's just the one, each visit the last. I've not known a sweet treat to tempt me like this one.

Some tips: Bake these from cold or even frozen. This will prevent them from spreading too much. For the same reason, don't flatten the dough balls before baking. These cookies are honestly still delicious even when they go totally pear-shaped—I've had them burned, underdone, way too flat, and way too thick (we don't know what goes on in the prep kitchen sometimes), and they're always addictive.

Makes 14 to 18 cookies

450 grams unsalted butter
300 grams dark brown sugar
225 grams granulated sugar
280 grams all-purpose flour
2½ teaspoons kosher salt
1 teaspoon baking soda

2 large eggs
3 large egg yolks
300 grams rolled oats
150 grams very light chocolate chips (we use Duleey 35% cacao from Valrhona)

First, brown the butter. It's not difficult, it just requires some vigilance at the stove and a little understanding of what's about to happen. Butter is made of butter solids and milk fat. If you've ever added butter to a pan that was too hot and forgotten about it, it's the solids that burn.

Caramelizing the solids without burning or separating the butter is invigorating. The butter emits a specific nutty, caramel aroma and it's delicious—on everything. Be warned, it's easy to go too far. The butter will keep cooking even when removed from the heat, so I recommend pulling it off the burner and continuing to stir at the very first indication of this alluring, distinct sweet-nutty scent.

Place a heavy-bottomed, deep 4- to 6-quart (3.8 to 5.7 L)) saucepan over medium-high heat. Add the butter and use a whisk to stir or swirl it every 30 seconds while it melts. Once melted, stir it constantly. The butter will start to foam a little bit. When it's foaming a lot, pay close attention, you must keep stirring. Keep your nose close to the saucepan and as soon as you smell the change in the butter, from regular butter to caramel and toasted nuts, pull it off the heat and keep stirring. It should be brown with some visible caramelized bits and the smell should be intoxicating. If it isn't quite there, you can slide it back over the heat for a few seconds at a time, while stirring. Set the hot butter aside to cool. A little warm is okay, but using it too hot will scramble the eggs, and that's bad. *(Recipe continues)*

While the butter cools, combine the sugars in a very large bowl. In a different large bowl, mix the flour, salt, and baking soda and set aside.

Once the butter cools a bit (to under 120°F [49°C], if you want to get nerdy), give it a stir and pour it into the sugars, scraping all the bits from the bottom of the saucepan. Start whisking. It'll be hard work and take a couple of minutes, but the butter and sugars will come together and it will smell warm and nutty and be quite tempting. It probably tastes delicious at this point, too, but who could say.

Add the eggs and yolks and keep whisking until everything incorporates as a whole, about 4 minutes.

If mixing by hand, add half the flour mixture and whisk until only a few white streaks persist. Add the rest and mix until just incorporated. You can use a stand mixer with the paddle attachment for about 4 minutes, but then you'll have to wash more dishes. If you're using a stand mixer, add the flour slowly on low speed. In both cases, be careful not to overmix; mixing should be minimal.

Use a rubber spatula to fold in the oats until evenly dispersed, then fold in the Dulcey chips. You could also add raisins or some dried fruit, or dark chocolate, but we omit any interference and opt for simply perfect oatmeal cookies.

Once the oats and Dulcey chips are folded in, the dough will be sticky and hard to shape. Stick the bowl of cookie dough in the fridge for 1 hour, and even up to a day. It'll be easier to work with.

When ready to bake, pull the dough from the fridge and preheat the oven to 375°F (190°C).

Once the dough has chilled to a workable temperature, roll it into balls. We like 75-gram portions, roughly the size of a regulation Ping-Pong ball. Place them on a baking sheet with plenty of room between each, 6 to 8 per large baking sheet—these spread quite a bit. You can use multiple sheets or bake in batches. If you're baking in batches, run some cold water over the baking sheet in between bakes so you're not putting the chilled dough on a hot surface. Bake for about 12 minutes and rotate the sheet pan. Bake for another 12 minutes, or until the edges are brown; the cookies may not look like they're done, but they're done. I admit that these can be fickle. Even the weird ones are great. They will spread out and crisp on the edges with a center that's very soft when they're done, and once they cool they are even better.

Rest on the baking sheet for 5 minutes before attempting to move them to a plate or your mouth. These are the kind of cookies that taste great hot, cool, one-day old, and also the following week, when you find a quarter of one left in a pastry bag in the pocket of a jacket or under your seat at a red light. Yep, still great.

TYLER'S BUTTERSCOTCH PUDDING

This pudding is a special treat that comes with some challenges: It can get grainy if you don't properly time adding the sugar and creates some ripe opportunities to potentially burn yourself; there are also going to be relentless requests once you do get it right because it's truly fantastic, so you'll have to risk it all again.

This is a great place to practice your custard prowess and learn about caramel. The custard is bolstered with cornstarch, which allows more room for mistakes because it has thickening power. You will, too, if you eat enough of this stuff.

Knowing how to make custard comes in handy when you encounter the need to make ice cream or crème brûlée. And two kinds of caramel, for when you need to throw the right kind in your enemy's face. You'll also be whipping cream, so you're a regular bon vivant (with a taste for revenge?).

It's a multipart recipe, and time-sensitive, so best to give it a read-through and get organized. When I'm making this recipe, in the heat of the crucial moments, you can find me commanding anyone in earshot to bring me a whisk or to help me strain, because I didn't get organized at the start. You could try that approach. Hasn't failed me yet!

Whipped Cream

240 grams (240 ml) heavy cream
1 tablespoon confectioners' sugar

Salty Caramel Sauce

100 grams granulated sugar
60 grams (60 ml) water
240 grams (240 ml) heavy cream
1 teaspoon flaky sea salt

Butterscotch Pudding

4 large egg yolks
1 large egg
40 grams cornstarch
225 grams brown sugar
75 grams filtered water
750 grams half-and-half
30 grams unsalted butter
Flaky sea salt, for finishing

Tools

2 large bowls
Stand mixer
Large heavy-bottomed saucepan with tall sides
Medium bowl
Whisk
Digital or candy thermometer
Rubber spatula
Ladle or pitcher for scooping hot liquid—
    a measuring cup works
Fine-mesh strainer

Make the whipped cream: Make sure your heavy cream is very cold and pour it into a large bowl. Add the confectioners' sugar and whisk till you get medium peaks—more structured than melted ice cream and you can dollop it, but not so firm that you could frost a cake with it. If you're whipping by hand, you'll know it's done when your arm falls off. Or use a stand mixer with the whisk attachment; go a minute or so on high. Do not overwhip! You can store whipped cream in the fridge for a few days, in something airtight.

Make the salty caramel sauce: Put the granulated sugar and water in the large saucepan over medium heat. Swirl a couple times but don't stir; stirring creates sugar crystals, which you do not want. *(Recipe continues)*

Let the mixture cook until you have large bubbles. It should be a rich brown and smell great, like caramelized sugar. Turn the heat off.

Carefully add the cream. It may bubble aggressively for a few seconds, then it'll calm down. It will solidify a little, and if you haven't done this before, you'll panic; don't worry. Just turn the heat back on to medium low and whisk until the sugar fully incorporates with the cream, about 2 minutes.

Pour the caramel into a heat-resistant vessel (not plastic!) and cool. Try a medium bowl, a roasting pan, or a baking dish. The deeper the vessel, the longer it will take to cool. True for all foodstuffs! Sprinkle the flaky salt over the top and fold it in. The caramel sauce will keep in the fridge in an airtight container for up to a week; just warm to pour. This sauce is also great over ice cream, or on Brussels sprouts, if you're chasing a Michelin star. Clean out your saucepan; we're about to use it again.

Make the butterscotch pudding: In a medium bowl, add the egg yolks, egg, and cornstarch. Whisk until incorporated and smooth. It will be thick. Set aside.

Add the brown sugar and water to the large saucepan and set over medium high. As soon as it's boiling, gently swirl the pan once or twice and return to the stovetop. Don't stir; it'll get grainy and then you're ruined. Be careful when swirling the pan: sugar gets hotter than boiling water and it burns way worse. Let the mixture bubble for 3 to 5 minutes, until the bubbles get big and you smell deeply caramelized sugar. If you have a thermometer, target 340°F (170°C).

Carefully add the half-and-half to the saucepan and whisk constantly. It will bubble up and the sugar may get a little stiff; just keep whisking over medium-high heat and it will all incorporate. Continue cooking over medium high until the mixture is around 130°F (55°C) on your thermometer.

Add a ladle of the hot butterscotch mixture to the egg mixture and whisk it a few times until mixed in, then continue, adding another ladle of hot butterscotch and again whisking a few times. Add one more ladleful and whisk; tempering, or bringing the eggs up to temperature slowly, protects the eggs from scrambling, the absolute kryptonite for this recipe.

Pour the entire mixture back into the saucepan and whisk constantly. As the mixture heats, it will thicken quickly. Pull it off the heat when you say, "That's pudding I would eat." Strain it into a large bowl through the fine-mesh strainer, using the spatula to force it through for maximum yield.

Add the butter and stir to fully incorporate. Put the bowl in the freezer or refrigerator, stirring every 5 to 8 minutes (so you don't get the dreaded pudding skin), until it's cooled.

Once cooled, transfer to a jar or airtight container, and cool in the fridge for at least 3 hours or up to 4 days.

When ready to serve, pour the pudding into small bowls, coffee cups, or little jars about two-thirds full. Top with salty caramel sauce and whipped cream. Sprinkle with flaky sea salt and serve to the great delight of your chosen guests.

GF PB AND JELLY COOKIES

You might remember when the new mega Whole Foods opened in Austin, Texas. I mean, who doesn't. It was 2005. It had a man-made creek, a public park (some tables you could sit at), ice skating in the winter, and, honestly, it was my favorite restaurant in town. I ate eleven meals a week there, maybe more. There was a sandwich called the Mopac, that thing was something else. But even that sandwich, with its guacamole and chipotle aioli and turkey and pepperoni (you had to be there), was a side note compared to an incredible gluten-free peanut butter cookie I discovered there. Those cookies inspired me, and I'm pretty proud of this recipe. Ours might be better (they definitely don't have any weird, unpronounceable ingredients in them). Sure you can make them without the jelly, no problem, but I think they're a total package.

Makes 14 to 18 cookies

720 grams almond flour
1 tablespoon kosher salt
1¾ teaspoons baking powder
400 grams peanut butter, creamy or chunky, that's a you decision; the natural stuff is best, but make sure to mix it well first
180 grams unsalted butter, at room temperature
260 grams brown sugar
240 grams granulated sugar
3 large eggs
1 large egg yolk
1 cup (325 g) jam of your choosing (optional): 1 tablespoon per cookie

Combine the almond flour, salt, and baking powder in a large bowl and set aside.

In a stand mixer with the paddle attachment (I've done some Luddite cooking in my day, but this one ain't worth doing by hand), cream the peanut butter, butter, and sugars on medium high until fluffy. You can also use a handheld mixer and mix the ingredients on medium-high speed in a large bowl.

Reduce the speed to low and add the eggs and yolk, one at a time, until each addition is fully mixed, 45 seconds for each addition.

Add the almond flour mixture in two to three batches, on medium speed, waiting until each addition is incorporated before adding more. There's no gluten, so we don't have to worry about overmixing. Mix for about 30 seconds after the last addition. If using a hand mixer, incorporate the flour mixture, in batches, with a wooden spoon or strong rubber spatula.

As with all cookies, it's helpful to chill the dough a bit before portioning and baking. This dough is a little slippery from the oil in the peanut butter so chilling is essential. Chill the dough, covered, in the fridge for at least 3 hours.

Once ready to bake, preheat the oven to 325°F (160°C). These bake at a lower temperature so they don't dry out or get too crispy; we want these soft and chewy.

Portion your cookie balls so they are between 75 to 80 grams. If you're eyeballing, aim for Ping-Pong ball size. Arrange on a baking sheet, and don't worry too much about space as long as they're not touching. Unlike the other cookies, smoosh these down a little bit to help them spread out. Give them a little gentle press with your hand so they are disc shaped and about 1 inch (2.5 cm) thick or a little less.

If you're adding jam, press your thumb into the middle of the cookie. Don't worry if the edges crack a bit. Place a dollop *(Recipe continues)*

(a tablespoon-ish) of jam on the thumbprint. Hell, if it's the holidays or a special occasion, you could even put a Hershey's kiss on that sonofabitch!

Bake for 10 minutes, then check them. I do a little push test close to the center to see if there's some give. Use your finger to press the cookie part very quick-like. When the center has some resistance about a quarter of the way down, take them out to rest and cool. Raw is no good, you'll know what that feels like, and if they have no give they're overdone. The cookies will cook a bit more once out of the oven. You can bake a little longer for crispy cookies if a crunch will cure what ails you. Cool them for 5 minutes on the baking sheet, then transfer to a rack or a plate to finish cooling, another 10 minutes or until you can't stand it anymore.

THE VOWS

Tyler asked me to marry him in February. We decided to get married in September. Of that same year. On a remote Italian island. All Time was in full swing and we were also building another restaurant. Curiously, coordinating forty of our closest friends to a foreign shore for a five-day party on three months' notice wasn't terribly daunting. But the vows . . .

When we got to planning, I asked him how we'd write our vows. Tyler told me quite matter-of-factly that he wasn't planning to write them. At all. I reframed the question, probing to confirm that he meant he'd memorize them—was I to do the same? No, he said, that's not what he meant. He said he would say all of the meaningful things about lifelong commitment à la minute—on the spot!—when they came to him. He would just devise them at our ceremony.

We were asking people to fly across oceans to witness our union and specifically celebrate us, so I thought there ought to be some kind of program. Tyler was nonplussed. Very "We're just cooking!" except sub "We're just getting married!" The competitive athlete in me—my note-taking, list-making self—was panicked. He would not be cracking a book before the exam; he would not be stretching his legs before the race.

I like a plan. I'm not extreme, but I do prefer to see a road map before the tires get rolling. If we establish a general direction, I have no issue with detours and snack stops—because we have a sense of where in the hell we're going. Usually, right as I am unfolding my proverbial map, Tyler revs the engine, does a smoky donut, and peels out. He likes to invent the path of travel once in motion. My map flies out the window.

This divergence between us isn't exclusive to the writing of vows. Tyler's creative process is so different from mine. It throws me off balance. Sometimes it terrifies me. In the middle of a tornado made of construction dust and other raw materials, all I can think is danger. But he sees something else—a possibility, the potential inside the mess. Right as I am on the verge of questioning or doubting or challenging him (or sometimes long after I have done so), something incredible happens. Our eight-foot ceilings are vaulted with perfectly laid, vertical-grain Douglas fir, or a twelve-foot table sits in our yard, or what was once an old, unused chicken coop becomes a cedar sauna, all by Tyler's hands. He's calculating and wholehearted, creating from a well of optimism and generosity. It's bottomless.

It's how he does everything, be it diving into a pool or braising a pork shoulder. He learns it while it's happening, fine-tuning midair or mid-sear, with impeccable precision and somehow simultaneously hurtling through space. He cooks like that, whipping up egg rolls and a cheesecake on Christmas Eve without ever having made them before. Tyler's workmanship, ability to learn something new quickly, far beyond the confines of the kitchen, and his attention to detail are unparalleled, but it's his openness that I admire.

I've come to realize over time that nothing he does is actually reckless. Though it spikes every red flag I've been wired to spot from childhood, Tyler's process is part of the harmony. I've found that the essence of something cannot come from the planning of it. The defining answers don't emerge from a plan but from the place where ideas and functionality and intention meet mistakes and nature and point of view and personal

experience and risk-taking. The path we're seeking is not revealed, it's forged. I know this is true, because we do it together, over and over.

In everything we make—restaurants, our home, our marriage, this book—we build a structure and then break free of it. Everything good happens inside that tension, in the place between the boundaries and the expanse. Like a Roman arch, the weight bears down, pushes out, and gives way to open space. That's our portal to freedom, to verdant pastures of creativity and collaboration. It's where the guts live.

In the early morning hours not long after our first official date, Tyler wrapped a piece of string around my ring finger while I was sleeping. Then, he carried a handmade ring in his pocket for three years, every day, so he could propose spontaneously.

On our wedding day, it was raining. The sea was chopping it up and the weather altered our outdoor plans. The thunder was loud, but my mom always insisted a storm was good luck on special occasions, so it made me feel peaceful and happy. I drank some tea and sat to write my vows on a piece of notebook paper, allowing them to come to me simply. I tore out the page and folded it up to carry down the aisle, my little map.

When Tyler took my hands and stepped toward me, in front of our family and friends, he lowered his voice and spoke so quietly it was indisputable that he was speaking only to me. So present and calm, he made his vows as he said he would, as he makes everything: from his heart, not from a page. Nothing he'd have written down on paper could have been as true.

SPECIAL THANKS

ASHLEY:

Since before this book project became a reality, I'd find myself driving to work writing the thank-you section of some future book in my head, in great detail. I would tear up. I should have written something down one of those times, but I didn't because there wasn't a book, and now here we are. I guess that speaks volumes about the magnitude of incredible people in my life to whom I am so grateful, find inspiration from, gain energy and support from, and so on. It'd be impossible to write a comprehensive thank you, as there's too much to say and too many to thank. Who come to mind immediately are the many people who have worked with us. From the beginning until this moment, so many talented passionate people have contributed not just to building All Time but to enlivening our lives. Some of our closest, deepest friendships have been born of the restaurant. To our entire team: I feel invested in each one of your journeys. I am honored to learn alongside you. You are the best team we have ever had, top to bottom. This place simply can't exist without you. Thank you for your energy, your generosity; thank you for showing up on holidays and regular days with a sense of humor and compassion. Oh my god, you make me laugh, you make me love coming in to work. Truly. Thank you, Leigh, for hanging with us and being so genuinely on board. Paul, you're one hell of a chef, cook, father, and friend. Frankie and Ferelith, you were there when we laid that first brick, you helped us define what All Time would become. Shout out to Jake and Will for sprinkling water on the invisible seedling that became this book. Thank you, Brandi, for believing in us, and for all of the support and guidance. Thank you, Marta and Lynne, for understanding our vision. Thank you, Craig, for bringing our ideas to life visually, and always with such little notice!

Thank you, Su, and thank you to Stephanie and the Harper team. To the AT community: Thank you for your evergreen support through thick and thin. Thank you for the grace and kindness you extend to our team. Thank you for remembering each of their names, treating them like they matter, for taking good care of them as much as you do us. Thank you for getting us, knowing us, loving us. We love you.

Christopher, you are incomparable, singular, beyond genius. Without your talent, your eye, and your intuitive understanding of us as individuals, and as a couple, this book and so much more just wouldn't be worthwhile. I can't imagine seeing through any lens but yours, ever, forever and ever. Grateful also to call you a dear friend.

Special thanks to In Lieu of Writing for all ceramics pictured in the book, handmade in Los Angeles.

To the spectacular, brilliant, compassionate women in my life, *friendship* is a piddly little word that can't encompass the sanctuary and essential wisdom, warmth, and strength that you impart to my existence. Your presence buoys me and allows me to more closely feel the presence of my mom. I love you so much, and I feel your love and support deeply. Life is cyclical, so at the guarantee of leaving out many important names, a few people have been formative in bringing this project to life: JD, you're a brilliant mind, a talented writer, and a hell of a friend. Thank you for returning all the inbox intrusions, late-night pings, panicked screenshots. You've gifted me with more knowledge, perspective, sage advice, good laughs, and grave truths than I care to list, and I know there will be more to come. Thank you for opening doors I never would have walked (or cantered) through without you.

Fra, thank you for bringing your rare breed of hospitality and unnamable creative substance to All Time. We are grateful to work with you and learn from you, but more than that, I am grateful for your friendship and for your spirit and energy and the magic you bring to our lives. Chien bisou. Ollie, you've infused life and beauty into so many corners of our home and work over the past couple years. What a wonder you are, thank you for your patience, vision, and for seeing the world the way you do. Kim, you've given me a priceless, lifelong gift, one that reaches way outside the confines of a ring. Thank you for teaching me about feel and balance and partnership. Still learning.

To the wine growers who have become friends, and the ones who were strangers but still welcomed me at your kitchen table, I have never been in more hospitable circumstances than when with you—always selfless, optimistic, simple, honest. There are too many of you to name, but to Arianna, Dani, Martha, Shaunt, Diego—our time together is always too short, but having cooked, laughed, eaten, and shared bottles with you fortifies me and inspires me daily, in my work and in my life.

To my brother, I love you. Thank you for supporting me and believing in me and listening to me so well.

To my husband: Thank you for teaching me how to shift, braise, smoke, chop wood, camp, sear, fix things, let go, get out there, get over myself, change the oil, change my attitude, know when to accelerate, know when to slow down; I am richer in so much—experiences, family, good books, stories, true friends, family, useful skills, unexpected knowledge, perspective, compassion, patience, clever jokes, and generosity—thanks to you. I am in awe of how you love, and not just me. You have expanded my capacity for life, people, nature, animals, Hudson, and ultimately, myself. I'm humbled every time you cook for me, every time you kiss our hound, and I love how you laugh and make me laugh. I am more honest because of you, more true and more open. Thank you for doing the work with me and for doing it without me. Thank you for being a builder and a dreamer and my partner. You are such a man. Thank you for always coming home. I sure do love you.

TYLER:
There are too many people to thank, really. I'm overcome with gratitude for our community, all of our friends, guests, supporters, farmers, vendors, and even the most confounding city in the country. I'm grateful for the dinners in our yard that validated that "just cooking" is actually so much more. If you know me, you know I'm a private guy when it comes to personal appreciation. Plus, Ashley hit all the tender notes above and I agree with her every sentiment. She says I still have to write something. So: To Matt Poley for showing me how to cook with soul and a point of view, thank you. To Melinda and Riley, the original backyard Sunday dinner crew, love you. To Travis, thanks for teaching me about timing and for not throwing the desk back. To Joe, thank you for supporting all my terrible ideas until one worked. To the team at All Time: we're nothing without you. To the best guests in the world: thank you for being invested in our business, our crew, our personal lives, Hudson's hobbies. To my beautiful wife who brought this book to life and a whole lot more, thank you for believing in me every day, even when I don't believe in myself. I am very, very grateful.

ABOUT THE AUTHORS

Ashley B. Wells is a hospitality professional, wine expert, writer, and restaurant owner. A Southern California native, she forged her career in hospitality as an alternate path when print journalists became an endangered species, around the time she graduated from USC with a master's in print journalism. She's run restaurants in Los Angeles for twelve years, has been named a *Zagat* 30 under 30, a *Wine Enthusiast* 40 under 40, and one of *Bon Appétit's* top six to watch along the way. In 2014 she founded Pour This, an online wine shop and subscription service she owned and operated for five years. Her writing has been published in *New York Magazine, GrubStreet, Life & Thyme, Vice, Terre,* and *Pipette.* Running service at the restaurant brings her joy, but when she's not at All Time she's probably riding her horse, reading, or sharing cheese with Hudson.

Tyler J. Wells loves cooking, but even more than that he loves feeding people. He's worked as an auto mechanic, a bicycle messenger, a construction manager, and a carpenter. He oversees the food and coffee programs at All Time, but he's also built the tables, made the shelves, ship-lapped the walls, and constructed and repaired nearly every corner of the restaurant he runs with his wife. He's consulted around the country, providing turnkey direction, conception, and operational guidance for award-winning hospitality programs. Born in West Virginia, he is a genius at making and doing and fixing, starting fires and cooking on them, driving, and much more. He is a knowledge seeker and a romantic and loves building things and being outdoors.

Tyler and Ashley (and Hudson) live in Los Angeles.

INDEX

Note: Page references in *italics* indicate photographs.